COOK'S (OLD SCHOOL HOUSE)

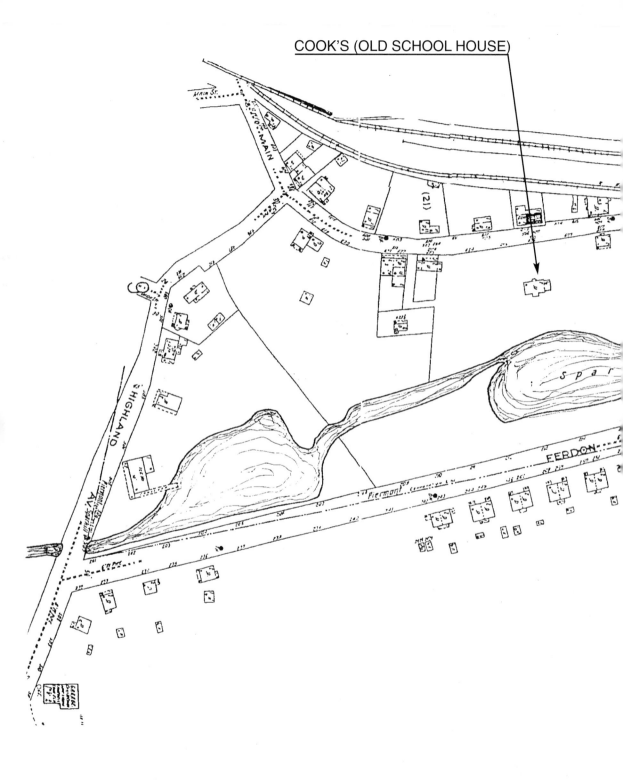

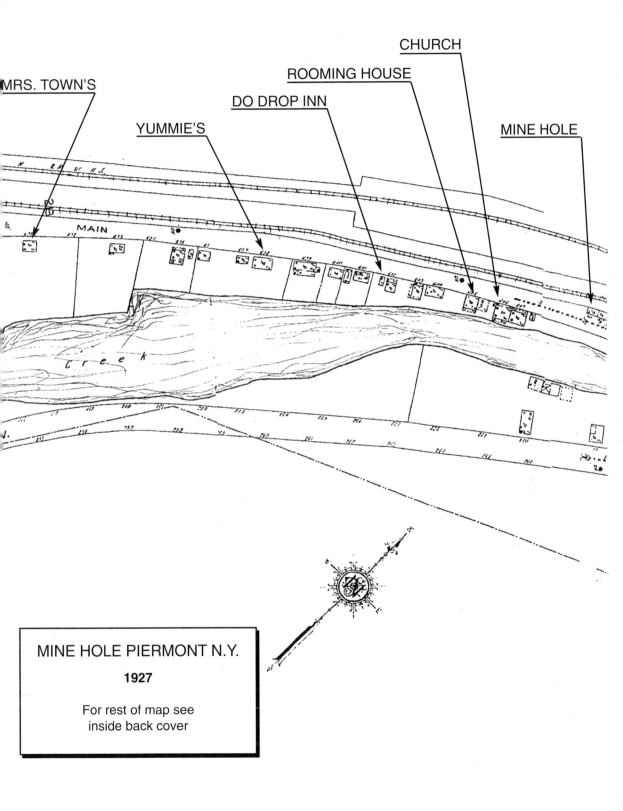

MRS. TOWN'S

YUMMIE'S

DO DROP INN

ROOMING HOUSE

CHURCH

MINE HOLE

MAIN

Creek

MINE HOLE PIERMONT N.Y.

1927

For rest of map see
inside back cover

About the Covers

The etching of the building alongside the Sparkill Creek, reproduced on the covers of this book, was done by the American artist, F. Townsend Morgan (1883—1965). The building included the famous double-decker outhouse.

The maps of Mine Hole inside the front and back covers were produced in 1927 by the Sanborn Map Company, the primary publisher of fire insurance maps for nearly 100 years. They are reproduced in this book with the permission of the Sanborn Library, LLC. Paul Melone adapted them to show the houses of some of the Mine Holers featured in the book, as identified by Benjamin W. Lawson, Jr.

About the Authors

Leonard C. Cooke's community service was concurrent with 32 years at General Motors in Tarrytown, N.Y., and continued for many years thereafter. In Nyack, N.Y., his efforts resulted in a water filtering plant, affordable housing, and a recreation building for the aging. He was president of the Nyack NAACP for ten years. His brilliance, high energy, and purpose were acknowledged by St. Dominic's College in giving him an honorary doctorate.

Audrey S. Lawson's early employment was in public and private social work. During her 20 years on the faculty of Adelphi University, she taught social work and African American history. In retirement her volunteer activities included service on the Governor's Advisory Council on Aging. A multitalented person, in 2003 she was voted Rockland County's Senior Citizen of the Year.

True Stories From Mine Hole

by Leonard C. Cooke and Audrey S. Lawson

Published by the Historical Society of Rockland County
20 Zukor Road, New City NY 10956

Library of Congress Cataloging-in-Publication Data

Cooke, Leonard C. (Leonard Charles), 1914-
    True stories from Mine Hole / by Leonard C. Cooke with Audrey S. Lawson
        p. cm.
    ISBN 0-911183-49-3 (pbk. : alk. paper)
    1. African Americans--New York (State)--Piermont--Biography--Anecdotes. 2. Piermont (N.Y.)--
    Biography--Anecdotes. I. Lawson, Audrey S. (Audrey Snypse), 1918-

    F129.P54 C66 2003
    974.7'28--dc21
    [B]

    2002032342

Volunteer Staff
Albon Man: *Editor*
Audrey S. Lawson: *Consultant*
Paul Melone: *Design*
Julie Jackson: *Prepress Production*
Jules Loh: *Copy Editor*

The Historical Society of Rockland County
20 Zukor Road
New City, N.Y. 10956
Phone: 845-634-9629
Email: info@RocklandHistory.org

TABLE OF CONTENTS

ACKNOWLEDGEMENTS

When an oral history is written down, it seems to us that the first acknowledgement should be to all those who have kept this piece of history alive. And so we salute first the oral historians of Mine Hole from the past. They made the recording of this piece of Rockland County history possible for many to enjoy.

Early on, with only a few pieces of our history hand-written on a yellow pad, we got enthusiastic support from a godchild and anthropologist, Professor Denise Oliver Velez. Wendy Snypse Belton, a now-deceased daughter, was equally supportive. Warren Halliburton, a novelist and old friend, offered some early positive guidance.

When the Historical Society of Rockland County chose to publish our book, we were blessed with help from Albon Man of the Society's Publications Committee. He brought many years of publishing experience, unbounded energy, and editorial skill laced with compassion and dedication in the pursuit of history. His contribution moved the book from a series of typed pages to a polished manuscript.

Julie Jackson, a Piermonter, generously volunteered to do the layout when our manuscript was completed. She herself is the author of a history of Piermont, and she wanted our unrecorded piece of Rockland's past to get into print. She was unstinting in contributing her experience in publishing, her computer skills, and her eye for marketing. We are grateful for her special talents, which gave us assurance that we would be proud of our book.

Paul Melone, with his background in book design, prepared the covers, adapted the Mine Hole maps inside the covers, participated in the layout, and took some photographs for us. We are thankful for his contributions.

We wish to express our appreciation to others, as well: Patricia Osterhoudt for her original photography, Harriet Smith and Karla Jones-Penn for typing the manuscript, Marie Koestler for her work on the computer disc, Arthur Iurica for steering us to the maps, Jules Loh for his exemplary proofreading, and the Piermont Public Library. Private collectors who made photographs available include: Howard and

Ruth Brawner, Leonard C. Cooke and Benjamin Lawson, George Lynch, and Frances G. Pellegrini.

We were encouraged to move past the manuscript stage of TRUE STORIES OF MINE HOLE by a most generous joint contribution one year ago from five Piermont residents. They prefer to remain anonymous. Though we cannot mention their names, their faith in the book and trust in us have been a constant inspiration.

Beyond all of this help has been the untiring support of our spouses, "Liz" and "Ben." Both have stood by with facts, ideas, an undaunted spirit, dedication, and love.

To so many. . .we are grateful.

> Leonard C. Cooke
> and
> Audrey S. Lawson

INTRODUCTION

There is a beautiful valley where the Palisades part briefly in New York to permit the Sparkill Creek to flow gently into the Hudson River. Snuggling on the north side of the creek, just about a mile inward, is the area known as Mine Hole. It's a small area, about half a mile long. It runs through the residential communities of Piermont and Sparkill, joining them into a solid, old community, rich in folklore.

A historical overview would reveal the usual story of the white settlers exploiting the Indians and struggles between the two groups, with the invaders ultimately taking over and dominating the area. We would like to pass over the events that fatten history books and, instead, feature the lives that are overlooked: the people who added color and vitality to Mine Hole.

Mine Hole is really a hole, seemingly man-made, in the mountain on the north side of the Sparkill Creek. Speculation has it that someone started to mine in this small area from which a lovely spring offered pure, cool water. Today, a sign mounted over its iron-gated entrance reads:

> O Traveler stay thy weary feet
> Drink of this fountain cool and sweet
> It flows for man and beast the same
> Then go thy way remembering still
> The well beneath the hill

Similar holes have been found elsewhere in the state, and one legend has it that they were dug by Norsemen as storage areas. Whatever the story, Mine Hole was a silent observer of the goings-on of a colorful, fun-loving, gambling, numbers-playing, bootlegging, religious, colored, Indian, Italian, sloven, dignified, ambitious and surviving folk.

Mine Hole had no professional or clerical folks living there in those times. It was a working-class and poverty group. The racial distribution of families was about two white to three colored. The families lived harmoniously together, cared about each other, and helped each other in crises. There was also a bit of interracial loving. The whites had a choice of other places to live, but the pattern of segregation confined the blacks to Mine Hole.

The colored population is the one we knew best and is therefore the focus of our stories. Many of the Mine Holers were born there. These were the traditional homeowners, established families, and were the traditional churchgoing conformists.

When the migration of coloreds from the South occurred in the '20s and '30s, laborers and domestic workers came in large numbers. They preceded the great migration of 1940 - 1970 when five million colored folks trekked north for a better life in the "Promised Land." Most of the locals who came to Mine Hole were recruited as strike-breakers at the local paper mill. The characters we write about were mainly of this group.

Our chief griot (an African word for storyteller), is Leonard C. Cooke, an 89-year-old African-American raised in Mine Hole and by a family with Rockland County roots. As an active little boy and keen observer, he was always in the street, dipping into everybody's business. We have the benefit of his memory of the good old days of the "twenties and thirties." His observations have been validated by other seniors who shared this scene.

Get a few of these old-time Mine Holers together and the stories start to fly. One begins spinning a yarn, another develops it, another corrects it and elaborates on a salient point. Collectively, they tell stories that just beg to be recorded. Two of us couldn't contain the urge any longer, for we feel time is running out and our remembrances are dimming. We dare to share them with you.

In writing any true story we think some descendants might be uncomfortable having family histories exposed. The Mine Holers we write about in detail are dead and we usually have used their nicknames. For a few, we have modified the names. Sarah Gaskins Cook and the Lawsons are untouched.

Those reading this book will bring many different lenses. Some will enjoy the characters; others will feel that more exposure of the less educated and less conforming folk will fuel the stereotyping of black people. We have to keep focused on the fact that the book is about life more than eighty years ago. The coping skills of people then may have been different from ours. No one has appointed us judge.

The impact of the civil rights movement and the ensuing positive changes cannot be denied. Images of our people have been modified by increased interaction with others in the workplace, in schools, in social situations, and in marriage.

Oprah, Colin Powell, Nelson Mandela, Tiger Woods, Denzel Washington, and the Williams sisters have taught the world that we are an achieving group. Dark-skinned bank clerks, firemen, policemen, teachers, and voting officials were largely nonexistent in Mine Hole's day. And the muscles of dark-skinned males produced paper in the mill and built roads and many buildings with us today. They are our ancestors whether we choose to recognize them or not.

Enjoy!

SAM BOSTON

It was a cool November morning in Mine Hole and out in the middle of the road was Sam Boston, screaming at the top of his lungs. "Some son-of-a-bitch stole my hams las' nigh'. If I catch 'em I'm gonna blow they head off." He meant it. Had his gun in front of him in position to blast in nothing flat. As he marched up and down the full length of road, he passed wooden clapboard, weather-beaten houses, some painted and some not. Some were neat, some falling down — private homes and rooming houses. His anger bounced against barber shops, a dance hall, the Dewdrop Inn, a store, pool hall and many legal and illegal businesses. The only road in Mine Hole was Piermont Avenue. The houses on Piermont Avenue were bound by the Sparkill Creek on one side or the railroad track on the other.

In his tirade, Sam was careful to avoid the droppings from the horses that pulled the wagons in 1928. He was hurt because he helped a lot of people; he was like an unofficial mayor. His ego was as big as his size of 6 feet 2 inches and 230 pounds — big in heart, size, and talent. His full-time job was a plumber but he was also an electrician, cement man, farmer, lover, handy man, engineer, and bootlegger. Want something done — ask Sam. He'd know how and the job would be done first-rate.

Front view of Bosco's rooming house. One of several places Sam Boston lived in Mine Hole.

Sam's talent probably gave him the confidence to come up North. He knew he could do all kinds of things and knew he could make it. One trouble overshadowed any move though — discrimination. The white man's anger over the progress made by coloreds after the Civil War caused many race riots in cities and many coloreds were killed.

Sam figured things would be better in a place like Mine Hole. And, then, damn it, there was trouble there like last night.

Sam was forever moving and at this time, he was living in a large three-story, wooden frame house with porches on the front and back. At that rooming house, Sam was up on the top floor. Everyone remembered it because its outhouses were different. The outhouses were at the same location, one on one floor and another directly above it on the next floor. Come to think of it, maybe you don't know what an outhouse is. It is just what the words say — a house that's out, therefore, away from the main house. Being that it was really a toilet without plumbing, it usually stunk and, therefore, was out — the further away the better. Usually you'd take a crap in the outhouse, use pages from a Sears Roebuck catalogue to wipe yourself, and both would land in a deep hole under the seat. A bucket of lime with a tin cup in it was on the floor in a corner for sprinkling over the droppings to make them sweet. It seldom worked.

Well, now you know what an outhouse is. Well, now figure out how they could set up two outhouses on outside porches at the exact same spot, one on one floor and one above it. How can two folks use them at the same time and not have to duck? First of all, there was no white sparkling seat as we know them today. The seat was only a slab of wood across one end with a hole to fit a behind. The trick here was that each hole had its own tin-lined chute to take the crap right into Sparkill Creek, which flowed into the Hudson. No stink there. Old timers will not eat fish from the creek even today. The state can stock it every year with perch, carp, sunfish, trout — doesn't matter. Locals know it was once an outlet for a toilet.

Getting back to the hams — when Sam slaughtered the hogs, everyone knew it. He used a saw mill a few steps away where there was a hoist for lifting them. Some fellows just loved to see the gory event and the word would be out. Sam's meat was the best — proven over the years. He'd soon have some for sale.

Gamble and Big Red got the word and, probably while into their usual drinking and playing cards, got an idea. They could make good money selling the hams. Much easier selling these hams than working in the tobacco and cotton fields down South, or getting 15 cents an hour in the local mill. Could have more money in the pocket for more gambling and liquor. Whiskey drinking dulled the Mine Hole rule they knew so well: You never crossed a person's door sill to steal. Well, anyway these hams were not past a door sill. They were outside on a porch — 15 to 20 of them. It was the middle of

These Piermont firemen and their nonmotorized fire wagon were typical of those at the time of Sam Boston's fire. The horse-drawn wagon pumped creek water. Photo courtesy Piermont Fire Department.

the night and all of the oil lamps were out. Big Red and Gamble quietly crossed the frozen creek, climbed up to the third floor, and handed down the hams and sold them in and out of Mine Hole.

Sam could cuss and threaten up and down the road all he wanted to — it all fell on deaf ears because too many would enjoy the good eating. Later that day, Sam was seen having a ham dinner at the Dewdrop Inn, Mine Hole's combination restaurant and dance hall. He really enjoyed his own ham.

At one point, Sam was living in a house, creek side. On a cold winter day, a small fire broke out. The white volunteer firemen were called. They really loved feeling good about themselves and had reason. They had good jobs, loved to party together, and usually included no non-whites in their exclusive fireman's club. Come to think of it, they were better known for getting pissy drunk than putting out fires. Beyond this incident, the whole community respected the service they gave.

3

At the firehouse, the whistle blew signaling a fire in Mine Hole. From the clanging of the bell on the red horse-drawn fire wagon, everyone knew they were on their way. Volunteers ran or rode horseback and they divided up the jobs. Some stretched out the hose from the fire wagon to the frozen creek, others cut a hole in the creek's ice to insert the hose, others attached the hose to the wagon itself. The fire wagon was not motorized, so four guys had to man the pump on the wagon to move the water from the creek to the fire. A couple of guys went inside Sam's place to check out the fire. They saw shelves of the pint-size mason jars filled with corn liquor. The fire fighting was over, it was party time. Of the 15 guys, 12 got drunk and went wild. One fell in the creek and, thank God, the fire was small and three sober guys put it out.

Feeling good — that was Sam Boston's purpose in life. The liquor helped, but he felt good in another way — feeling the power of money. A piece of the action — a big piece. It motivated him to work hard on his full-time job as a plumber, playing the numbers heavily, being the best bootlegger, selling the best butchered pork and vegetables, taking risks, and doing odd jobs through new ideas and talents. He was a doggone winner any way you look at it. Get that money and take it to the bank, watch it grow. Getting ahead —happiness!

Everyone's night out at the bank was Friday. It was open late to accommodate the crowd. The biggest employer was the local mill, and Friday was payday, and the pay was by check. There were three shifts and the bank opened four or five windows and some six to eight people would be in the lines at each window. This was also the biggest racial mix anywhere. Churches generally were segregated; on the job there was segregation. Folks outside Mine Hole had little mixing of the races, but come Friday night it all hung out at the bank.

Sam was wearing his daily uniform — a clean pair of overalls with the bib front. He held his raunchy cap, which he usually wore pulled to one side, in his hands. Being a respectable gentlemen in those days meant your head was uncovered when you were inside. Quietly awaiting his turn, he thought: I got more money on me then most around me, colored or white. Damn right! A lot more than those white bitches — the tellers. Yet I couldn't get her job 'cause my color ain't right.

That's okay, I can hack it. I got plenty of money. Can't keep me down.

In line behind him was a poor excuse for a man, a small, frail twerp of a white man. He held his straw brimmed hat in his hand and was dressed in a cheap checkered suit, a starched white shirt, and a polka-dot tie. The tension was obvious in his upturned nose as he kept his distance, a good two feet behind Sam.

Sam stepped up to the window. The power of money so deeply entrenched in Sam's being was full blown at this point. His pride as a man and as a colored man soared as he slowly, meticulously, retrieved rolls of money from his various pockets. No one in the bank stopped work, but there was a bit of slowdown as other white folks glanced over to take a fleeting inventory. The white tellers were accustomed to this uppity nigger depositing all this money, and so were the colored who lived near him. Mr. White Sharp Ass was in total disbelief and moved closer. Sam was well aware of his presence. As Sam slowly, deliberately emptied another pocket, he moved closer and ended up almost on Sam's back. Money had erased the distance between them — for the moment.

Sam the Victor had won again. Displaying his money on Friday night, right in the money institution of the community — the bank. Sam's power was on parade. Sam was a winner.

"Sam Boston" was a nickname. In pinochle or bid whist, you win the whole game if you take all the tricks with one hand. It was called "running a Boston," a term popular today. Sam "ran many Bostons" in life and one of his tops was making the best corn liquor any-where. Step into Mine Hole anytime and you could smell his still cooking. During the entire time of prohibition, 13 years from 1920 to 1933 and after, Sam offered a community service making whiskey, got rich, and had plenty for himself — 'cause he loved some whiskey, legal or illegal.

He was a top flight plumber, so you'd figure he'd make only a top flight still. He would take a big metal container, say the size of a garbage pail, with a good-fitting top, make a hole in it and solder a long piece of copper tubing to it. He'd coil the tubing around several times, and then lead it down into a vat. In that large container, he'd boil mash or corn and water and the steam from the boiling traveled up the coils and condensed. As it cooled, it ran into the vat at 150 proof. In today's stores, most whiskey is 86 proof. Sam's whiskey was some powerful stuff. You could get drunk just smelling the stuff. Sam "cut" the proof and stored it in pint mason jars for selling.

Like most migrants, Sam never bought a house. He liked living in rooming houses. But Sam did rent one house that's standing today. Out back he built a shed just for his still. He knew how to run a gas line from the house to the still and all was working well. His wife had died, and he was tomcatting around and got hooked up with a beautiful young woman. She was two-timing him with a young soldier who found out. The soldier stormed up to Boston's house, ordered him out doors, and a bloody fight was on. The chick sided with the soldier, took out a knife and stabbed Sam nearly to death. Blood ran in the street like water. The police came and took Sam first to the hospital and then to jail. While Sam was in jail, the still cooked on and on. The liquor was smelling stronger and stronger. Everyone got scared.

Cornbread said, *Damn thing might blow up, then what?*
Gamble added, *No liquor? No smiles.*
Tiger Flowers remembered, *The shed door's locked!*
Dee-Troit said, *Man — Let's call the police and at least shut it off.*
Gamble thought: *Sam'll get arrested?*
Dee-Troit reminded them, *Someone'll get hurt if it explodes.*
They all agreed to call the police.

Well, the police came before that still blew. They sawed off the padlock to enter the shack, turned off the gas under the cooker, and went back to the police station. No one ever heard another word about it. Neither did Sam.

The woman who did the stabbing? She and Sam got back together and had a long relationship. More fighting, more loving, more cutting, more making up, more black eyes, more kisses until they moved to Pittsburgh and out of sight.

TIGER FLOWERS

It was a beautiful quiet spring morning in Mine Hole and a pretty little girl was walking east toward the sunrise when out from between two houses stepped Tiger Flowers. The child took off like a bat out of hell and left Tiger yelling painfully, "Don't run away lil' girl. I wouldn't hurt you for nothin'. Tiger Flowers' a nice man."

Briefly, that summed up Tiger Flowers. He was one hideous look-ing man and he tried to overcome it by being nice. The scars from an old knife wound divided up his black face beginning under one ear, cross to the other side, and from one eye down to his lip and left his

Benjamin W. Lawson, whose chickens were stolen by Tiger Flowers, Mine Hole's Robin Hood.

face a horrible mess. Some people with African blood develop keloids. Keloids are a thickening of a cut area, and as it heals it bulges, making it pop up, widen and look even more ugly. Tiger Flowers had many keloids. Not only did children run from him but adults turned away as well. Just the nickname "Tiger Flowers" gave many messages. You had to be a tiger to survive those knife wounds and yet, soft, sweet and appealing like a flower to survive among people who'd like to run away from you.

On the other hand, maybe he chose the nickname "Tiger Flowers" because it was the name of the very first colored boxer to win the middleweight championship — a highly respected and popular guy at that time.

The fact that Tiger chose a boxer's name at all reached back into slavery with pride. For entertainment, the masters selected a slave or two to represent their plantation in boxing matches. Being chosen probably meant you were in the best physical condition from a group of very physical men. You were given special treatment, like the best of foods, more training time, and less time picking cotton. You could travel outside the plantation.

7

Colored migrants of the '20s and '30s were first generation out of slavery. Most of their parents were slaves and many were still alive at the time. In fact, boxing was to these migrants what basketball is today to young black people in the inner city and everywhere today. A way out. One way to get rich, own big cars, have fine clothes, pretty women, furs, diamonds, and money in the pocket. Lots of money.

Pride and interest in boxing were influenced further by a nearby training camp for boxers. National celebrities like Primo Carnera, Jack Sharkey, and Kid Chocolate (colored) worked out there frequently. And then there was a local colored semipro by the name of "Mexican Joe" Lawson. He would drop in and out of Mine Hole. He'd fought Jack Sharkey and loved bragging about the good life. The success of colored heavyweight champion Joe Louis was all over radio, and the celebrating in the streets caught on everywhere.

While dreaming of becoming a boxer, Tiger Flowers' day by day life was one of hard work in construction — building the railroad, roads and buildings, during the day and drinking liquor into the night. He'd even make money drinking liquor. He'd bet he could gulp down Sam Boston's 150 proof stuff in one gulp — never lowering that pint mason jar from his mouth 'til it was finished. And he could. His musclebound, tall, lean, body would be erect and not wobble one bit when he'd leave the scene of such bets. He'd leave happy with money stuffed into his pockets.

Making connections with folks was hard for Tiger. Couldn't get or hold a woman for nothing. Depended on Mrs. Town's "Ladies of the Night" for an hour or so. He made a few friends with men. He was a more passive type than a troublemaker. He made his best connections by being nice to those in need, stealing what they needed. Drop in, listen to a sad story, and Tiger would help find a way out. So there were two chances to make connections — one to check out need, the other to deliver the goods. Steal someone's chickens, rob a garden, get coal from a coal yard, whatever. He never thought much about the right and wrong in stealing, but more about helping his neighbor. He felt good being the Mine Hole Robin Hood.

Ben Lawson's chicken coop (across the creek) was large and filled with about a hundred prime chickens. In a glance across the creek, one could see them pecking away in their fenced areas invitingly. Lawson had noticed a few chickens were missing and decided he'd alert the lone Piermont policeman, who would get a backup from the state police if needed.

"Take from the rich — give to the poor" was Tiger's motto. Well the nearest "rich" people were the Lawsons, and no matter that they were colored. Stealing was an "equal opportunity" opportunity. They lived on the other side of the creek and owned all the land that paralleled Mine Hole. They were the second generation of free colored ancestry — a big contrast to the strikebreakers' crowd. A number of the migrants worked for the Lawsons and knew their property quite well, probably casing the joint for the future. Tiger figured it was no problem to steal from the Lawsons. It was not stealing from inside the house — a Mine Hole taboo. Lawsons weren't in Mine Hole anyway. Thought they were better than everyone. Stuck up, churchgoing hinkty niggers — another term for folks who thought they were elite.

Tiger Flowers got Foots, a fellow migrant, to help him make a raid. They had gotten a couple of burlap crocker sacks to carry the load back to Mine Hole. The night was pitch black and clear. It was on the weekend when party noises were loud and might help drown out other noises. Tiger Flowers and Foots made their way over the bridge and down into the Lawsons' yard. There was no lock on the gate or hen house. The chickens started to cluck, not too loud, but enough to let Lawson know something was wrong so he better call the police. Tiger was inside the hen house handing the chickens out to Foots standing outside at the door, who dropped the chickens into the bag. No conversation on either side. When the policeman arrived, he took Foots' place, and Tiger, not even looking, handed the chickens out through the door into the policeman's hand. He was arrested. That's where Mine Hole's Tiger and Sherwood Forest's Robin Hood differed.

In the Lawsons' household over the years, a tradition developed of having folks over for eggnog during the Christmas season. The Lawsons were conforming churchgoing folks, as were those invited for eggnog. Just a few years ago, one of the guests began speaking of events in the past, how great Tiger Flowers was during hard times. How he came to the house to see what the need was, coal, chickens, whatever was needed. Lawson Junior interrupted the story: "Yes, he brought you chickens, all right — ours." That was a complete surprise to that guest. As a child, she'd been eating Lawsons' chickens. Folks fell out with laughter.

"Laughing to keep from crying" is an old term used by coloreds and I guess others who are underdogs. Whenever a few Mine Holers get together over the years they tell these stories and in the laughter find relief from the pain. Tiger Flowers is one of the first characters remembered in these story-sharing sessions.

MRS. TOWN

Big. That's right, big. Think of Mrs. Town and you think big. She was big in size, had a big bulldog, lived in a big house, and only the big gambling games were at her joint. And the spirit around her place was big — like a Las Vegas of Mine Hole. That's it. Just like Las Vegas. There was gambling, but all the other added attractions, too. She had bootleg liquor for sale by the shot. There was good food, of course. On the weekend, you could count on three or four prostitutes — beautiful colored women who were equal opportunity ladies and who came from other places.

Mrs. Town was a strong, light-skinned, heavy, muscular, and aggressive woman feared by both men and women. She'd beat up a man if need be, and she had many a backup system. There was a big club she left on the porch for emergencies. She carried a big switchblade knife.

Mrs. Town's constant companion was a bulldog as feisty as its mistress. Photograph courtesy Emanuel Topal.

It was the common assault weapon during the 1920s. Her bulldog was at her side all the time, ready to attack at her command. The women of Mine Hole had few chances to work. Some took in washing and ironing for wealthy whites nearby and some were domestics in the wealthy white homes. In contrast, Mrs. Town was her own boss, and she was damn good at it.

Folks can't pinpoint just when she came to Mine Hole from New Jersey. Seemed like she was always there with her husband Johnny, a skinny, childlike, passive guy with a wooden leg. Although he worked regularly as a janitor, he had time to help her out in the bar or the kitchen.

She had a bar in that house, part of which is still standing today. The porch ran across the front and on the right inside there was a large room that had the bar, table and chairs, piano, Victrola, and a dance floor. That was during Prohibition. Having liquor displayed at her place was really one bad-ass move because this was during Prohibition and alcohol was illegal. During the week, there was a player piano. On the weekend, that room on the right would have a live band. The dancing and the partying were loud and lively, and the "ladies of the evening" would make their contacts there. These attractive young women were busy. Mrs. Town took a percentage of their take and provided the bedrooms upstairs and one or two bedrooms on the first floor. Her adopted 13-year-old son would often invite his friends to view the action through a torn window shade on the first floor bedroom. Free.

On the front left side of the house was the gambling room. A big old bare oval table dominated the room and hanging on a chain above it was a large kerosene lamp. There was no electricity in those days. Eight or nine gamblers sat on the chairs which were seldom cool, because everyone standing around was waiting to get into the game. In fact, those standing usually had another gambling game going on — betting with each other about what was going to happen at the table. At the table, the usual game was skin — an explosive, fast-moving card game in which the matching of cards was the main idea. Most of the gamblers were the migrants, and that room was the scene of many arguments and bloody battles.

Mrs. Town kept on top of every piece of her operation, but cutting the gambling games really made her rich. Cutting the game meant taking part of the money. Sometimes she'd announce the amount she was going to take. That depended on her whim, or the size of the pot. Sometimes she might just reach in and take a hunk of money. If you raised a stink, you'd get put out. But if someone got broke playing she just might give that person $5 to get him back into the game and keep things moving. One smart business woman.

"Okay, Cornbread. Your luck seems bad tonight," said Mrs. Town as she gave him $5 to stay in the game. This boss lady had just taken an akimbo view of the situation. In other words, she used an African woman's stance in decision making. Standing with her feet apart, hands on her hips with the palms opened and turned back so this decision was given in an authoritative way.

No operation like Mrs. Town's could go unnoticed. In fact, even though everyone was gambling all over Mine Hole and drinking illegal whiskey as well, it was all on a small scale and less of a deal. Piermont had only one police officer, and he was probably tired of being made

Mounted state police like these came down the street seemingly to enforce the law at Mrs. Town's house of many illegal doings. Photograph courtesy New York State Police.

to look like a fool with all that illegal stuff going down, so he got help from the state police. You had to be 6 feet tall to qualify for state police work, so when 16 big white brutes, handsomely dressed and handsomely armed, rode their equally impressive horses two by two down the road, everyone's eyes turned and mouths flew open. It was a once-in-a-lifetime event. They went and surrounded the house.

It was late on a hot summer Saturday night, music was blaring out the windows, the prostitutes were making their moves, gambling was in full swing, and all the folks had been drinking and feeling no pain. The joint was jumping. When the police surrounded the house everything stopped. It got so quiet you could hear a mouse piss on cotton. No music, no clinking of glasses, no creaking of beds, no rattling of change. Everything stopped. First, the police concentrated on the gambling room so they could pocket all the money in view. They ordered all the men to get up, face the wall, and put their hands up on the wall. They were quick about it except for Gar Lawson. Gar had been crippled when kicked by a horse in childhood, and though he was trying to get up, he was not quick enough for the police, and they proceeded to beat him up unmercifully. Sound familiar?

Gar was no Uncle Tom or to put it another way, he was no passive lackey like the Uncle Tom in Harriet Beecher Stowe's book. He had the backing of a highly respected family and he brought a suit against the police for brutality and won a good settlement.

A strange thing about this incident. That was the first and last and only time Mrs. Town's ever got raided.

DEE-TROIT

In 1920 a labor recruiter from Piermont down in North Carolina looking for strikebreakers would select the biggest, toughest guys, because these guys might have to use force to cross the local workers' picket line. Inside the mill, the work was hard and the hours long. Toughness was a must. Moving away from home and family was another drain, but these guys were hungry for money and a chance to work to get ahead.

It's a fact that Dee-Troit was the toughest man to land in Mine Hole. That toughness was a reason he was selected as a strikebreaker. But his stock was probably rooted in a couple of generations of tough slave stock. The slaves survived, and so would he.

The mill paid 15 cents an hour, and in time, some muscle men like Dee-Troit left the mill for better money in construction. There's migrant sweat in the soil of Route 9W, the railroads, and many of the buildings. Dee-Troit worked with one of the biggest construction outfits around. The hauling wagons were pulled by a team of horses. To drop a load, you had to pull a lever which opened the bottom of the wagon bed. The contents fell into a hole. Once, a wagon had just released a load

This paper mill actually sent recruiters into the South to hire strikebreakers. Dee-Troit was among those recruited. He was among the toughest of the tough in Mine Hole.

into a pit and was pulling off when a back wheel started to slip into the hole. Dee-Troit grabbed a spoke of the wheel, braced his body against the hole, screamed out, and held it until the horses were able to make another start in pulling the wagon out.

Another time, a crew of tough guys were digging out a foundation for a building, and in Rockland County, there were rocks everywhere underneath the soil. Plant a garden — rocks. Plant a tree — rocks. And every construction job meant rock removal. Sometimes it was easier to build around or over a big rock. The choice might be to dig a large hole and push the boulders into it then continue the building on top of it. That was the plan when they hit a big boulder say about 8 feet by 4 feet. Dee-Troit was digging in that hole to make it larger when the boulder gave way and moved toward him. He braced himself against the sides of the hole and with his feet held the boulder off alone until others heard his screams and came to help before it crushed him to death.

Dee-Troit's muscles made him extra money after work. Keeping warm in those cruel winters of the '20s and '30s was tough. It was too expensive to buy coal by the truckload. The only way to survive was to buy hot or stolen coal from a smarty like Dee-Troit. There was a whole business that centered around gathering places like barber shops, pool halls, beauty shops, and bars. If you wanted a hot item, you placed an order for the brand, designer, size, and color of the item you wanted, and had it delivered at 30 percent of cost or less. One of the biggest hot items in Mine Hole was coal.

Mine Hole was on the other side of the tracks. The railroad ran right beside it and carried coal in open freight cars. There was a railroad spur in the nearby coal yard. Trains uncoupled and cars stopped inside the area with a 10-foot fence. The coal yard owners put six German shepherd guard dogs behind the fence to keep out burglars. Dee-Troit brought these dogs food every night, talked with them, and stroked them. His new furry friends were so glad to see him each evening that their tails wagged. He earned their quiet cooperation.

With his orders in mind — 50 cents a bag — he developed a good hot coal business. He would throw empty burlap bags over the fence, scale the 10-foot fence, fill the bags, throw them back over or climb back over the fence with the bag on his back, and carry them to those most in need. At each door, no one person had the strength to lift the bag into the house. Two had to do the job or they'd make two trips with one-half of a bag.

Dee-Troit's interest in making money was paramount so he served everyone, those with money and those with little money. It's safe to assume that there were a few with no money; we'd guess he didn't pass them by.

There was one family with six children and an unemployed father who came to the door. "Dee-Troit, man can't tell you how much getting this coal means. Been so cold I took to burning up some of the floor boards. Here's a dollar." He then called three of his older boys to help him get the bags inside.

Mine Hole survivors were just that, survivors. Times were tough and the pattern of surviving depended upon many parts cooperating to make a whole. Dee-Troit was a vital part of the pattern.

Gambling was nonstop in Mine Hole. Mrs. Town's was for highrollers — those with the most talent and money. Small card games or crap games sprung up all the time behind the barber shop, in anyone's house, or anyplace. Numbers playing made gambling easy because there were so many numbers writers around. For a penny or two you could keep a dream alive any time, all day.

"Yummie's Place," a rooming house and gathering place, was for mid-weight gamblers. It was open every day and almost every hour of the day. Yummie himself looked and acted the part

---

Journal News

NYACK, NEW YORK, FRIDAY, JULY 24, 1925

PLANE CIRCLES OVER NYACK TO ADVERTISE KLAN

Drops Slips Reminding Public Of Parade And Carnival At Suffern Tonight And Tomorrow; Buttons And Ribbons Being Sold On Streets; Many From Here Plan To Attend First K.K.K. Public Function In Rockland County.

Nyack, N. Y., July 24—The arrival of an aeroplane distributing in cloud-like lots slips bearing in read ink "K. K. K. Suffern, N. Y. Saturday, July 25, 1925," and the distribution of small buttons bearing an imprint of the American flag and, suspended, a small ribbon on which is printed "100% American," against the Klan cross as a background, all combined to greatly stimulate the keen interest being shown today in the Ku Klux Klan Karnival which opens tonight at Tallmans, and continues tomorrow with a parade of 3,000 members in Suffern.

Shortly after eight o'clock last night the plane made its first appearance, winging towards Nyack over Bradley's Hill. When the plane, which was about 1,000 feet up, got over the center of the town a flood of small slips of paper, resembling in the distance a cloud of smoke, were let loose.

The papers scattered as they fell, and many were carried out over the river. Enough fell in Nyack, however, to inform the whole town just what the mysterious aviator's mission was. There was a scramble for the slips as they fell in the streets.

Later in the evening a group of men and women, who arrived in automobiles, began selling the small buttons and ribbons, as described above. It is not believed that these people had anything to do with the Klan organization according to statements made

this morning by authorized representatives of the Knights of the Invisible Empire.

The carnival, for which extensive arrangements have been made, opens tonight in a large field a short distance from the center of Tallmans. Booths, similar to those maintained at firemens' carnivals, have been erected. The Klansmen and members of the womens' organization, the Kamelias, are expected to wear their regalia, but no masks.

Tomorrow evening at six o'clock, the parade will take place in Suffern. Streets of that village, they will parade to the carnival grounds, where addresses are to be given by speakers of national importance. Dancing, and other entertaining features will be on the program. The general public will be welcome. No passes will be required. Three hundred members of the Klan from Nyack are expected to be in the line.

The KKK was active in these environs as seen in this newspaper article. Cross burning, even as a prank, is unsettling. Newsclipping courtesy Craig Long.

of a gambler in a 1920 movie. He was tall, thin, good-looking, well-liked, light-skinned, and smartly dressed. Garters held up his sleeves and his long slim fingers were manicured to perfection. These fingers knew how to shuffle the cards fast and use the art of "palming." Palming is another term for stacking the deck. Yummie could take a deck of cards and in the shuffling arrange the cards so he'd win most of the time. He'd let a few guys win, once in a while, to suck others in.

Another big attraction was his wife's cooking, including the favorites — fried chicken, pig feet, a pot of chitterlings, cornbread, potato salad and sweet potato pie. There was good money to be made on the food and whiskey that were sold.

A small group of guys were playing skin when Big Red came in breathlessly screaming, "They's burning a cross up on the hill. Must be 20 guys in white sheets and hoods with eyes cut out so'se they can see to shoot straight. Nerve to be singing 'Onward Christian Soldiers.' Whitey's no damn good."

"Yeah, they's some mean suckers and burning the cross to say 'Nigger stay in yo' place'," suggested Yummie.

The card players thought they had left that crap down South. They knew there was segregation up North — going to the movies, not getting certain jobs and spots on school teams. But in Piermont the bars and restaurants were for all, children went to school together, and everyone shopped at the same stores. There was no time to sort it out bit by bit. Some sons of bitches had burned a cross — right in view so the colored could see it.

Everything stopped. The guys jumped up and bolted out of the door, going for their pistols, shotguns, rifles, whatever. The word spread. Others joined them and up the hill they ran screaming and shooting. When they got to the cross, no one was there. As the cross finished burning Dee-Troit spoke about a lynching he'd seen down South.

"Framed this guy, saying he'd disrespected a white woman. Then they threw a rope over a tree limb, with that rope hung him by the neck, cut off his 'thing' and poured kerosene over his body and burned it up."

Big Red added, "What's worse, white people usta come in cars and chartered trains just to see a lynching. They tell me some three thousands

19

The very mention of KKK called up real images of lynching like this one for immigrants from the South. Photograph courtesy the Allen Littlefield Collections.

been lynched. Makes me sick!"

Gamble chimed in, "But I still say there's something fishy about the whole thing. We's up North and Piermont ain't like that." As the men came down the hill talking, they felt a certain sense of relief and success.

Dee-Troit said, "We's up North and we fought back. Makes you feel better when you can fight back and maybe win sometimes."

Gamble suggested, "Yeah, let's see whose gonna win that game of skin we left."

The next day in school, some of Leonard Cooke's white "friends" shared their story. The day before a newspaper reported that in Suffern, a town about 13 miles away, a cross had been burned by the Ku Klux Klan. These "friends" thought it would be fun to try it in Piermont. They had gotten two 2x4s, formed a cross 15 feet high, and soaked it with kerosene. Then they wrapped the cross with white sheets, added more kerosene, and set it afire. They marched and danced around the cross and sang to attract attention.

The fact that Cooke saw the burning cross as a prank by "friends" is interesting. "They didn't do this to be mean," he says even today.

Cross burning is a racist, negative act that upsets any community — colored or white, in Mine Hole or out. For the Southern colored folks looking for a better life up North it was an especially tough experience. Nevertheless, they talked about it, faced the reality of the act and went on with their daily activities of coping and surviving. When facing life's uncertainty, an old slave expression describes it best: "Just keep on keeping on."

BOB POWELL

Up North was the Promised Land. Things were supposed to be different there. Better. One of the ways for getting ahead was having power. Voting was the thing to do. Bob Powell and George Astwood regularly read the Amsterdam News — a colored paper out of New York City. They knew that there had once been a colored governor of

Pond Lily was not a pond or a lily, but the home of Bob Powell and the site of parties, more drinking, some skin games, good times and all kinds of stuff.

Louisiana. There had also been colored lieutenant governors in Mississippi, South Carolina, and Louisiana. Coloreds had also been elected to state offices in a number of other states. People began to think Rockland had to get its act together. Get to voting so we can get some respect.

Up North there was no poll tax like down South. It didn't cost money to vote. Down there they had crazy rules; like you could vote only if your grandfather had voted. Most of the folks were slaves and didn't have voting grandfathers. Sometimes colored voters also had to recite the Constitution of the United States.

21

The KKK, burning torches in hand, would yell and ride horseback into the colored sections just to scare folks. Sometimes some of them would be armed and they'd shoot a person or two — for control. And of course, there was lynching. Some of the prejudice carried over to Piermont where colored voters were sometimes asked a lot of unnecessary questions. They'd be frightened and walk out. Not being scared by these tactics, George and Bob showed leadership smarts and were tapped by the Democrats and Republicans. At different times, they were connected to both parties depending upon who paid the most at the time.

Bob also was head of the biggest numbers operation in Mine Hole, operating out of "Pond Lily," a strange looking, long skinny building like a railroad car. It was one jumping party place. Lots of Sam Boston's whiskey for sale there.

Bob loved to drink and beat up on his women. The first chick was Lucy, a thick, short woman. She wasn't too bad looking, but later she was pushed out by Lillie — a tall, thin beauty. Every Saturday night Bob would get drunk and flail away. His blows and the woman's screams were so loud you could hear them across the creek a hundred feet away even in the winter when the windows were closed.

Showing off beating up on women or showing off with the kids in the street was Bob's thing. At 300 pounds, he was a big six-footer with a huge, hard belly that he invited the kids to take swings at like a punching bag. He never flinched but roared with laughter. He was a well-liked meriney. A meriney is a colored person with a bleached out reddish look. With their thick lips, flat nose and kinky hair, they looked like other coloreds.

Somehow, Bob seemed very comfortable with white people outside Mine Hole and hung out with them. They had power, and he could get into the political machine through them. Might get more for himself and his folks. The other person comfortable with the whites outside Mine Hole was George Astwood. And maybe he had the same idea as Bob. Living at Mrs. Town's, he was more active at the far end of Mine Hole.

22   George was a handsome, light-skinned guy with beautiful mixed

gray hair. His hair was straight like the white man's. "White is right — nigger get back" was a popular saying among coloreds then. Coloreds thought to be white was to be a winner. So having white or light skin tone, and having straight or near straight hair, meant the person was more like whites and, therefore, good.

In the thirties, George had an office job in Nyack and worked for the Works Projects Administration. He was a smooth, intelligent guy with political smarts. Sometimes he was a Democrat and sometimes Republican. Whoever paid him the most got his service.

At election time, George and Bob really worked Mine Hole. They were slapping folks on the back, shaking hands, smiling, and talking their talk. Indian, white, colored, old, young everyone was a possible voter. Bob and George were in full force.

They even got the kids into the act. The children got an adult's small wagon they could pull themselves. On one side, they'd have Republican posters, bunting, and pictures, and on the other side they'd have the Democrat's stuff. They'd beat an empty pan as a drum to call attention to themselves. In the downtown section of Piermont, the Republican side of the wagon would pass the Republican headquarters, and the Democrat side would pass the Democrat headquarters. They'd stop in for and get a tip from each party.

The adults, urged on by George and Bob, went first to the Democratic headquarters and collected $2. Then they went on to the Republican headquarters and collected $2. Finally on Election Day they voted as they damned well pleased.

SARAH GASKINS COOK

Late one night, there was a banging on Sarah Gaskins Cook's door. Some woman in Mine Hole was having a baby, and Sarah was the midwife.

Sarah Gaskins Cook, midwife and healer.

She jumped out of bed, pulled on her clothes, and got into a waiting horse-drawn carriage. She tried to calm the worried husband and away they went. Usually the deliveries were manageable for Sarah, but sometimes the local doctor had to lend a hand. When all was over, Sarah was brought back to her home — a former school house.

The Cooks' home during the earliest years was a few feet off the main road in Mine Hole, down the slope and quite close to the Sparkill creek. Tallman, Sarah's husband, was waiting there. He was 15 to 20 years older and when he saw Sarah as a kid he called her an "ugly pickaninny." Pickaninny meant a colored child and was an affectionate word. After his first wife died in childbirth and Sarah had grown up, he married her and together they had eight children. The nearby state park was named Tallman after a rich white man. There's a question about a possible blood relationship to the Cooks, a free family. Just as in slavery, the blacks working for whites often took the family's name. Some of the Cooks did work for Tallman, and some were very light-skinned.

Sarah was a pretty, tiny woman about 5 feet tall and weighed about 115 pounds when Tallman married her. Part Indian and part African, she was not only a midwife but the community healer for everyone. Didn't matter to her what color of skin the sick person was. Didn't matter if they were churchgoing or not. Anyone sick was her personal worry. She'd make house calls to rooming houses to tend migrants, sober or drunk. There was no charge, but a gift wasn't refused. Everyone respected her and called her Mom. The toughs with vulgar mouths would get a swift kick to shut up if they were sounding off when she walked by.

Sarah was not the only healer in Mine Hole. The other local healer in Mine Hole was Mrs. Oscar, one who worked roots. She was known to gather roots in the woods or on the side of the road and to order them by mail. One day Sarah saw her stripping bark from a sassafras tree nearby and asked, "Where do you usually get your roots?"

Mrs. Oscar replied, "Well, sometimes I go into Harlem to shop. Mainly, though, I shop by mail through the colored papers. Now they's got ads for everything including healers who remove hexes, restore

The Cooks' home, which was once a school building, was a Mine Hole landmark.

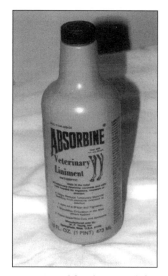

Liniment like this, used for horses and people — then and now.

nature, give good numbers and use voodoo."

Some places with strong African traditions also had witch doctors. As close as Brooklyn, witch doctors, also called natural doctors, used roots, animal blood, feathers, dolls, pins, and spirits when they can cast spells or remove them. Children sometimes wore "asphidity" bags to drive away evil spirits. From a string around the neck, a cloth bag about the size of a large postage stamp held the asafoetida herb. These bags stunk and kept folks away. Can't vouch for the evil spirits.

Another source of help for sickness in Sarah's day were the medicine shows at the annual local fair. Usually one man would set up a booth with bottles of stuff to cure just about any ailment. He'd hawk his wares, making a lot of outrageous claims. Most of the locals were wise to these guys, but a few tried the medicine. Cheaper than going to doctors and less scary.

But Sarah was not into any of these remedies. She had plenty of others, mostly stuff around the house. When the leaves would start to turn color in the fall, it was time to make goose grease. Tallman would get the biggest goose from Bosses' store, some 20 pounds or more. The fatter the better. In those days, fowl were not cleaned, so Sarah operated on the goose like a surgeon. After taking out the guts, she'd separate the bile from the liver and destroy it. If the bile bag broke, everything it touched would be bitter. The heart, the liver, and gizzard were set aside for giblet gravy. The butcher had scalded the goose and removed most of the feathers, but those left were tough at the neck, legs, and the tail. Once the feathers were off, some fine hairs remained and had to be singed over an open flame.

Washed, dressed and propped on a rack in the pan, the goose was ready to be cooked slowly. The grease settled at the bottom of the pan and was gathered during the cooking. When cooled, that grease was solid and used all during the winter. You'd put goose grease on flannel on your chest and it would surely cure a bad cold.

Sharing the goose grease was a good Christian, prideful thing for Sarah. Tiger Flowers got the full treatment when he took sick. She gave him goose grease for the chest. She made him some onion syrup for his cough by boiling one cup of water, adding an onion, one-half cup of sugar and cooking until a syrup was formed.

Other cold remedies included drinking a cup of hot tea with honey and whiskey. A few drops of kerosene on sugar was another cough suppressant.

Johnnie Cooke came into the house with severely frostbitten ears. Sarah soaked white potato slices in kerosene, fashioned them into cups that fit over the ears and taped them in place overnight. This drew out the pain and the ear turned black for a day or two.

Little Mary had a nasty boil under her arm and Sarah's advice was to break an egg and apply the thin skin that is inside the shell. This drew the infection to the top and when poked with a sterilized needle, the pus popped out. A needle was sterilized by burning the end until it turned red.

Sterilized needles were used to pick out splinters, but when this failed, Sarah suggested taping a piece of salt meat, like bacon or salt pork, to the spot at bedtime. By morning the salt in the pork would have drawn the splinter out.

Brown soap douches for abortions, horse liniment for sore muscles and sassafras tea for a spring cleanout are among a few we can recall. There were many more remedies we cannot now remember. Enough to fill a book.

POP SMITH

Pop Smith was over 6 feet tall and seemed 6 feet wide. Worked on construction, even built the now famous Route 9W which runs from Englewood Cliffs, New Jersey, to Albany, New York. His muscles were probably developed through two or three generations of hard work in slavery. He was one of the many real toughs in town. Pop was safe in Mine Hole because his strength was respected.

Strangers were always dropping in and out of Mine Hole. After all, there was plenty of action there, of all types. The fact was, the more folks came and went, meant the more money in town. That was the way those in business saw it. Two outsiders got tangled up with Pop Smith and they stabbed him. They realized from his power to fight back that they'd better cut out. They hauled ass, ran like hell and were never seen again. This fight was not the rule though. Folks didn't mess with that bundle of power — Pop Smith.

Toughness made it easy for Pop to run a successful gambling place. He cut the game. No question. Just having a place for a game meant a lot. Not having to worry about the rain, snow, heat, or cold, having light, and being away from the snooping church folks was good. Pop had a rented house with migrant men as roomers upstairs. The gambling in one room on the first floor was not as frequent or profitable as at Mrs. Town's or Yummie's joints, but it was fairly steady. His location at one end of Mine Hole made him a big shot there.

Pop Smith had two defining characteristics: his derby and his big cigars. Laborers and those in the lowest class didn't wear derbies. Sporting types like those around the race track, undertakers, and gamblers wore a derby.

Smoking a big Cuban cigar was more uppity than cigarettes. The size and price of cigars signaled that you were a step above everyone else. That's the picture Pop wanted to get over, and he did.

Pop stepped out on the porch one summer day and saw Giuseppe — a steady huckster who had nice fresh vegetables on his truck. As usual, a couple of street kids followed him and when he wasn't looking, they'd push off a few fruits so they'd roll down the hill out of sight. They'd get them later.

In those days, Mine Hole was crawling with hucksters. One after another all day long someone was selling something from the back of a horse-drawn wagon. Vegetables, fruits, meat, fish, pots and pans, or even dry goods like linens, dishcloths, bolts of material, thread and the like. Another daily huckster, of a sort, was the numbers writer, selling a chance to get rich. Another salesman was the insurance man. For 10 cents a week, he would guarantee a decent burial pay. But hucksters were different. They'd sing out their wares, or yell or clang a bell or gong to get people to come out. Items were sometimes a little cheaper since the hucksters didn't have rent to pay.

Giuseppe was in a pushing mood. Pop had bought a few vegetables and while he was adding up what he owed, Giuseppe pressed on again. "Want some delicious bananas? Cheap!"

"No," Pop said.

"A real good bargain."

"Now I done tole you I don't want no damn bananas," Pop said. Pop took the four-foot stalk of bananas and threw it into the creek, dusted off his hands, and went back into his house. Back to his money making — cutting the game.

Guiseppe turned his truck around and went right to the police station as quickly as he could.

The one policemen in Piermont was a sad excuse for a man. He was small, frail, flamfooted, and he couldn't balance himself on a motorcycle. He used one with a side car attached to keep his balance.

The lone policeman in Piermont at the time had a tough job. Misbehavior was everywhere.

When the white police were sizing up a situation, they'd come alone. But if it was time for an arrest, they'd bring along additional white guys they'd deputized or they'd get the state police. That lone policeman stepped up on the porch and knocked on the door and quickly stepped off the porch, waiting on ground level with Guiseppe. They both knew well Pop's strength.

"What the hell you want?" Pop barked.

The policeman spoke in the toughest voice he could get out. "Now you know it wasn't right throwing those bananas in the creek."

"Listen, let me tell you one damn thing. If you don't go over and climb up on that tricycle and get the hell out of here, I'll throw you and the tricycle into the creek."

They both left.

Whether Pop was right or wrong, no doubt about it, Pop felt good. Up North he could tell off a white policeman who just might have been a Ku Klux Klan member. When the white man's heel is on your neck day and day out, not letting you breathe and treating you like a dog in slavery, your need to feel like a man is great. The need to tell him off is liberation.

REV. EDWARD JONES

The whites were no angels either. They were into lots of drinking, gambling, fighting, and sleeping around as well. The first do-gooder was a white man with a little money and a missionary spirit. He built a Catholic church. It was aimed at those sinning white folks since coloreds didn't much follow Catholic churches. He put up a small white building. Masses and programs were held. They tried hard to slow the roll of sin, but they failed.

In a short while, along came the second do-gooder missionary type — colored Reverend Edward Jones — a jackleg preacher. A jackleg preacher was one with little formal education who knew a lot about the Bible and was independent and connected to no one. He announced that he had received the call to preach. The jackleg preacher himself decided when and if God spoke to him, and he had received the call.

Reverend Jones learned down South that the sinning he saw in Mine Hole was going to land a lot of people in hell. They'd have been better off if they'd lived a more Christian life. They knew better. They had learned what was right and wrong before they got up North. In fact, their parents told them what their slave parents knew from the Southern preachers on the plantations, since worshipping God was the only thing slaves could do besides work.

The plantation owner also owned the preachers — white and black. He'd let them read the Bible, do some preaching, and sing slave songs. The songs were about how things would be better by and by when they'd get to heaven. It gave the slaves comfort and hope and kept them under control.

Reverend Edward Jones was not really owned by anyone. A small, brown-skinned man, he worked in construction and carried himself with dignity. He liked a sip or two of Sam Boston's corn liquor from time to time, and had no wife but a girlfriend. He was respected and thought that a church situated right in Mine Hole might make it easy for sinners to come in and get saved. St. Charles A.M.E. Zion Church was too far away — a quarter of a mile. And their members were too sa-did-dee, which means you think you're cute and better than the sinning crowd. Reverend Jones also heard that a few folks were meeting in a home trying to start a Baptist Church. There was no need to wait for them, and who knew where they'd put the church. There was an empty church right in the middle of a hell hole. He thought he would be pleasing to the Lord, and the offering plate might have a few dollars for him.

Reverend Jones went to the man who put up the Catholic church and worked out a deal. He got a few folks to help him take down the

This church, originally built as a Catholic church, was later reestablished by Rev. Edward Jones, a jackleg preacher who said he received his call directly from God.

statues and the gold and glitter, because coloreds liked things plain. When they pray, nothing should get between God and the prayer. Serious business.

In thinking about himself as a new preacher, Reverend Jones knew he lived a clean life and folks wouldn't question him. He knew the

Bible up and down and in and out. No one knew more about the Bible than he. He knew what chapters certain verses came from. Because he was a good actor, few knew he was illiterate. The members weren't the questioning type anyway. Don't question a person with the call because that wouldn't be respectful. Might bring on bad luck or something.

Colored churches were as varied as colored folks themselves. Some were formal, with well-educated ministers and got connected to a national group. Others just popped up with a well-meaning leader as a minister, and they liked the independence. Some churches leaned on reason; some leaned on emotion.

Reverend Jones' church was the emotional type. They were holy and sanctified. Another name was holy rollers because they'd get happy with the Holy Spirit and roll on the floor. Back then, some churches put sawdust on the floor so the roll would be more comfortable. Many churches threw sheets over the ladies so if their skirts move up too high in the rolling they would remain decent.

Every move anyone made in Mine Hole was everybody's business, so to start a church you didn't need flyers, posters, or announcements on the radio. The word was out and a few folks admiring Reverend Jones and his idea came and joined up. The church gatherings would be led first by a church member. They began low-key and quiet, and someone would get up and speak personally about how good God had been to them. Someone else might lead a spiritual or two, another would testify again about the goodness of God, and a prayer or two would be offered. That was the warm-up for the main event, led by the preacher.

When Reverend Jones took over, the once-quiet gathering got loud, filled with the Holy Ghost. There would be singing, drumming, shaking of tambourines, dancing, prancing, praising, talking in unknown tongues and flailing of the total body even to rolling on the floor. Talking in tongues was a babbling kind of talking that was unknown, strange, and might have been spoken when a person was into the Holy Ghost spirit. The person seemed out of his head, and in another world.

Revival was a special event — a time when the preacher made a special effort to save souls. Sometimes guests speakers and singers would come. Usually it was a three- or four-day event, sometimes a solid week. That was when the Holy Spirit really took over and souls were saved.

Reverend Jones had announced the spring revival and folks came out better than usual. Among them were some pesky teens who wanted entertainment. They had been part of the foot-washing ceremony and were deep into the throes of rolling on the floor wrapped in sheets. Lo and behold, a Mine Hole father like the devil in the flesh came into the church, not with a pitchfork but a stick. He marched right up front and began beating on the teens. They quickly gained "consciousness" and ran home like HELL!

The church members enjoyed the fellowship, the everlasting hope of Christianity, and the status of being among good folk. The Baptist church, which had begun formation in homes, got established just outside of Mine Hole. Reverend Jones' effort at church organization only lasted a couple of years. There wasn't a formal count of members but no doubt his efforts were weakened by the establishment of the Baptist church.

DOT

On a beautiful Sunday morning in spring, Dot woke up bright and cheery, ready for a full day in church. Her church, St. Charles A.M.E. Zion, was nothing like Reverend Jones' Mine Hole church. This congregation was founded some 100 years earlier by a group of free coloreds in Skunk Hollow, an area a couple of miles away. They later moved to a site one-fourth mile from Mine Hole. Their minister could read, had some formal education, and was sent by the national body of the African Methodist Episcopal Zion Church. The services were less emotional and quieter.

Dot jumped out of bed, cleaned her teeth, and washed her face. She had had her bath on Saturday night in a large, round tin tub used for washing clothes during the week. She put the tub on the kitchen floor near the stove to keep her naked brown body warm. Then she filled it with water warmed on the stove. There were no bathrooms during the early '20s in Mine Hole. She'd finished washing up and put on her underclothes, which included a corset with eight metal

There were no bathrooms in Mine Hole. For a bathtub, Dot and other Mine Holers used a large galvanized washtub like this one by the kitchen stove.

stays to help it keep its shape. She'd had a cup of coffee, put on her floor-length dress, and began fixing her hair. She first covered her shoulders to keep her outfit clean. The night before she had greased her hair with pressing oil and ironed out the kinks using a heavy metal comb she'd heated on the stove. She was careful to get into the kitchen (another name for the nape of the neck), since kinks in the hair could be stubborn.

On Sunday morning, just before leaving for church, she would unroll her curlers — kid curlers. Kid curlers were about 3 inches long and 1 inch wide and made of kid leather. Inside was a piece of heavy wire. The leather grabbed the straightened hair, and the wire inside gave it more control for curling. Kid curlers were the most expensive. Some folks used heavy wire curlers. If you were poor, you folded strips of paper from brown paper bags.

Dot used a hot metal comb and a dab of hair grease to make her kinky hair straight, a beauty treatment.

Those kid curlers had done a good job. Dot had arranged her hair and then topped it off with a fancy hat, and pulled on her long shawl and gloves. With a pocketbook in one hand, she picked up a platter of homemade cookies. She was ready for church. She brought the cookies for the Mission Society's Annual Sisters' Tea after the service. She and her sisters would have one table. She was looking good for the tea and for Mr. Burton. He'd come by for some action later, she was sure.

Having a tea was a very special thing in the colored church. People dressed up, enjoyed the refreshments, and heard the locals perform. There might be a reading, a piano solo, a recitation, or songs by an individual or group. The colored church didn't usually like dancing. Most importantly, the tea was a sure way for talent to be seen and get started. The tea was also a fund-raiser. At the silver tea, people left a piece of silver money. For an eagle tea you would leave at least 50 cents — a coin with an eagle on it. It was a nice way to spend Sunday afternoon.

The tea was a time for church women to be as elegant as their white lady bosses. The tables were beautiful — lace tablecloths, fresh flowers, candles, and a silver plate service for tea or coffee and dainty china cups and saucers. Finger foods were served on platters. A plate with a doily held a little change, inviting others to add to it. Two ladies would be tea pourers — one at one end of the table and one at the other. They'd be looking as sa-did-dee as they could — nose tilted up a bit and speaking only in quiet tones. To pour tea meant you were a classy leader. Dot was chosen pourer for that tea.

The teas attracted more women then men, but one church leader was on hand for every event — Mr. Burton. Dressed in his Sunday best, blue suit, white shirt, striped tie, his 5 feet 6 inch 170 pound frame was looking fine. A father of five and a grandfather to 15, he was sashaying around like a rooster in a hen house. His eyes caught Dot briefly. As a church leader, he had a chance to do there what he couldn't do anywhere else — be in charge, and run things without the white man dipping in. At the tea, he was on the fringe, but a leader is a leader.

As a member of the Board of Trustees, he knew the inner workings of the church — its budget and its money-raising efforts. Now the tea was OK; so were the church fairs and selling chicken dinners. The two best money raisers were Mr. Wills' clam chowder sales and the gospel concerts.

Mr. Wills, an old member, had moved down into Jersey someplace, but once a year he returned to make and sell Manhattan clam chowder for the church. He'd use an oval, galvanized wash tub that was about 2 feet wide and 3 feet high. His recipe was a secret, but he was seen opening 350 clams, chopping 6 pounds of beef brisket and 3 pounds of salt pork and peeling one and a half pecks of potatoes.

People came from everywhere. They'd line up with little metal lunch buckets and jars to carry the chowder home. This annual event helped fill the church coffers.

The gospel concerts were the best fund-raisers though. The regular church choir sang the old favorite hymns, and so hearing a rousing group of high-spirited singers was a treat. About 15 locals would unite to sing twice a year. They'd sing loud, use tambourines, drums, sticks, clap, shout, dance and praise.

The concerts would last a week, and the 25-cents admission was enough to meet the church budget for the year ñ the preacher's salary, the heat, light, postage, whatever. White and colored folks lined up early to get seats. Quartet singers and soloists in concert would draw a fair crowd, but these gospel concerts were unbelievable.

As the tea drew to a close, Mr. Burton helped put the tables and chairs back in place, saw to it that the doors were locked, and made his way down the road.

Back home after tea, Dot smiled because she knew Burton would be coming by. Although he was a little man, he was well endowed. Their coming together would be copasetic, a fine, satisfying, special thing. Dot removed her hat, and placed it in a box. Passing the mirror again, she got another reminder. She really was one ugly broad. She was about 5 feet 6 inches and not too fat, but her broad flat nose was a mess. She'd had a nose job done and it was worse than before. She wondered again if Joe, her husband, left her because she was so ugly. Or because they had no children. Or maybe he found out she was sleeping around. They had a comfortable home, and she worked for wealthy whites whose leftover antiques made it nice. She was a good cook. These thoughts made her sad. She missed Joe and she wasn't making any new connections she could count on.

The whole Mine Hole was run over with sex. If someone left the front door unlocked they might pass their living room and find someone making out on their couch, their floor, or in their hall. The urge was great. Getting it on was the only thing on their mind. Dot was seen doing it outdoors behind the billboard, behind a shed, in a garage or anywhere, anytime, just carried away. It was never enough for Dot. She was totally into sex. It was a wonder she never got pregnant. The term teenage pregnancy wasn't often used in those days. There was one woman who was the chief abortionist. She used a coat hanger or a shoe buttonhook to open it up so air could get in. Then everything inside would come out. That was followed by a warm douche of Octagon or any brown soap with lye and all would be well till the next month.

Dot was one sad woman. Her deep, sincere church life was not enough to keep her straight — forever lonely, forever a sexaholic. Toward the end of her life she was ill and had to go on welfare. When she passed away, she was still a loser. Folks came into her home and helped themselves to her small valuables and the antiques gathered from whitey's houses over the years. Her white social service worker pulled up a truck and moved the larger antique pieces to his wife's antiques shop on Route 45 in Spring Valley.

Dot — a loser in life and after death.

CURLIE

An Indian in Mine Hole? He didn't know — Curlie didn't know much of anything about himself. We doubted he was a pure-blooded Indian because his black coarse straight hair had a little curl in it, like it had a touch of colored blood. But he was about 6 feet 2 inches, lean, straight as an arrow, had high cheekbones, deep-set eyes, thin lips, and he had red-brown skin color. He wasn't the only Indian, or mostly Indian, to show up in Mine Hole, but he was the only one to live there a long time, marry a colored woman, and buy a house.

The Indians and coloreds married often. They felt close because they had a common enemy — Mr. Charlie, the white man. Whitey took their land and treated them like dirt; whitey took the coloreds' freedom. Naturally, they'd feel close to each other. Over the years, before Emancipation, the Indians helped the slaves when they wanted to escape to freedom. They'd hide them in their homes, guide them at night through strange fields and mountains, and then connect them with safe places to stay. Some slaves stayed on with the Indians. So when Curlie came to Mine Hole from Warwick, New York, looking for work, he landed in a place full of coloreds knowing he'd be with friendly folks.

There was another thing that pointed to his being more Indian than most. It was a well known fact that Indians did not fear heights. He worked on the tall buildings of Rockland Psychiatric Center and later the Tappan Zee Bridge. Much later he got some kind of award for the fearless scaffolding work on the bridge as a foreman. He fit that mold of being mostly Indian. In those days, people's idea of "mostly Indian" came from cowboy and Indian movies. Still, he had a sour, unsmiling look on his face all the time, didn't speak when he saw you, and kind of looked through you rather than at you. That only fed the prejudice.

Curlie was by himself most of the time. His favorite things were hunting and fishing at night alone, except for the two large hound dogs he'd trained to hunt 'coons. He made a killing catching 'coons. Good food — good furs for sale.

Although he was a feared loner, Curlie loved to gamble, drink, and play skin, which caused him to mix with Mine Holers. At a small pick-up game in a house one day, a group was deep into gambling. Curlie, Dee-Troit, Gamble, and Blue had put in several hours and Blue was leaving. In those days, there was at least one Blue in just about every colored neighborhood. Blue was the nickname of a very black-skinned person, so black that the skin gave off a blue tint.

Curlie's knife was 9 inches long when he pushed the button to release the blade.

A dark skin can also appear to have an ash-like film easily removed by a dab of spit, Vaseline, lard, oil and — when you could afford it — Jergen's Lotion. Another option was bleaching the skin with a product called Nadinola. Blue couldn't change — too black and too poor.

A tough construction worker, Blue was small by Mine Hole standards, probably only 150 pounds and 5-1/2 feet tall. He loved to gamble but he hated to lose his money. He'd been deep into a game. He was leaving, got mad, went outside, and was raising hell. He was cursing loud and began throwing rocks at the house, breaking windows. Curlie had had a few drinks. He got tired and came storming out of the house. He pulled up his pants leg, took his switchblade knife out of his long sock, pushed the button and the blade popped out. He grabbed Blue, sat on a rock, flipped him across his lap and stabbed him in the butt, yelling, "Take that, nigger. When you gonna act right, anyhow? Don't know what's the matter wif you!"

Blue was shocked the Indian had grabbed him. He jumped up and began screaming and crying. He put his hand on his butt and felt the blood. Sure enough, the Indian had stabbed him. More screaming and crying. A crowd gathered. Curlie called out for some iodine, adhesive, and clean rags for bandages. Someone brought the stuff and Curlie pulled Blue's pants down and bandaged the wounds. Blue tucked his tail, straightened up, and flew right for a long time. The card game continued.

BILL JACKSON

The Depression was a bitch. There's an old colored expression about hard times — "When white men catch cold, colored men get pneumonia." Well, during the Depression, Mine Hole was full of pneumonia. Jobs were hard to find. In the relief agencies, Jim Crow was alive, giving surplus grapefruit to the coloreds and surplus 2-pound cans of hams and roast beef to whites. There was some seasonal farm work at 2 dollars a day for a 10- to 11-hour day of very hard work. Rockland County was farm land in those days, so there was some work, but it was seasonal.

The mill where the Southern blacks came to work as strikebreakers kept open, but on a low level. Whites and colored had been laid off. At one point, the word went out that the mill was hiring. Over 500 men showed up for three jobs and two were filled by past employees. The mill, the biggest employer in Piermont, was divided along race lines. The nice clean work closer to Piermont's center was the box factory that hired all white except for Ben Lawson, who was in security at the gate. He looked "light, bright, and half white." In the eyes of some, he passed for white. The dirty work was in the paper factory close by but farther out toward the pier, away from the town's center. There the employees were mostly colored. When the Depression came, it hit everyone. It was an equal opportunity unemployer.

Survival was built into the colored man's lifestyle, and it took a whipping during the Depression. To make it, they'd have a small garden patch for vegetables. They'd eat some and can some. Then they knew how to work the butcher for free things like pork chitterlings, chicken feet, hearts, livers, gizzards, and the ends of cold cuts. For a few pennies a pound, they'd get chicken backs and wings.

Another freebie was fishing and crabbing in the Hudson. Without pollution, the fishing was great. Striped bass, Lafayettes, eels, blues, perch, and catfish were the good eating from the pier. Coloreds survived on their catches.

The coloreds had two supports — hope and playing the numbers. Riding on top of the numbers crest was Bill Jackson, the numbers runner. The runner was the one who collected the number slips from the local writers and "ran" them to a colored banker in Jersey. The banker Bill used for a long time was murdered in a mob deal. Still, Mine Hole was running over with numbers writers. After all, it was a job. Soldier Boy, Harry Powell, and Mrs. Sutter were busy all day writing the numbers. Bill did some numbers writing himself.

Bill was the ugliest man in Mine Hole. His dark skin was covered with deep holes left from smallpox. He was the son of the second ugliest man in Mine Hole. They both had dark skin, little, beady, black eyes, wide flat noses, and thin lips. At 5 o'clock, it was time to gather in the slips because they had to be in Jersey right away. The number came out at seven.

In making his rounds, Bill had been to see Sam Boston's wife early in the day and had doubled back later. Now that was one lucky broad, but then again she studied the numbers and seemed to have figured out how to win.

Mrs. Boston had studied the dream books from front to back. A dream book tells you what numbers will come out if you dream such and such. "Policy Pete's Dream Book" had listed every dream in alphabetical order with the right number listed beside it. "Three Wise Men Dream Book" had a summary of how often certain numbers hit and a listing of the hits by the month. Numbers were matched with names, items dreamed about, days of the week, and hunches. A hunch might be losing your laundry and the number listed as 864. Being cheated by someone was listed as 483. If someone liked a particular number, they could look it up and there was a listing of the month and date that number usually hit. Sister Boston studied a few of these many books, which kept her busy all day.

She was a big fat momma, weighing nearly 300 pounds, and loved sprawling out in a big chair with her feet propped up on a footstool. The stool was pretty fancy for a stool and covered with a printed, lush material. When she died they found out why it was so fancy. It had over $40,000 in it. Numbers winnings were in the stool — the bank.

Another stop Bill would make was Mr. Gates' pool hall where money was both in the pool game and the numbers action. Dee-Troit

Dreambook hunches were the mainstay for Bill Johnson's numbers-playing clients. The game involved painstaking research.

got a hot tip from Dot who shared the hymn number sung in that night's prayer meeting. He felt confident in the number because an angel had told him to play it.

Big Red remembered that his house number came out almost this time last year so when he saw it on the license plate of a passing car he knew it would win. With such a good hunch he decided to play it heavily. Then again, he thought he'd play it with more than one writer because sometimes they'd cheat. They'd claim that the cops caught them or some other excuse. By spreading the bets around it might be safer. Endless time and energy were spent figuring what numbers to play.

One former Mine Holer's mother played a number only just before Christmas and it always came out. Her kids never forgot it because it meant some good extras, including Christmas toys. That number's so deep in that family life today, the children and grandchildren call when they see it come up in New York or New Jersey. Of course, it was played. Of course it hit. Can't give the number — might break the spell.

In those days, people would know the winning numbers by word of mouth, the radio, or the Daily News. The number was based on one of two things. For a time, it was the last three numbers of the total

earnings of the stock market that day. Another time, the number was tied to the race track. The winning jockey's number in the first race was the first number of the three played. The jockey's number in the second race was the second number, etc. Folks would huddle around the radio listening to the results. Some folks only played on one race, the first race, called the Boleada. The whole numbers playing deal was unending.

These number slips of Cooke are still in his wallet. The numbers have been revised here because publishing them might taint their magic.

The payoff was great. One penny might have made you $5 richer. One dollar might have gotten you $500. During the Depression, a $5 win was a lot of money.

On October 27, 1933, Cooke played two numbers. One for $5 and one for $1. That's 70 years ago, and in his wallet today is the numbers slip, browned with age. He's been playing those two numbers off and on for all these years and will tell you how lucky he has been. Quietly he has played those two numbers in two now-legal state lotteries. He won't tell you what they are for there is a magical quality. If someone learns what they are, it might break the spell. The magic will evaporate. Dedicated numbers players will never reveal their numbers.

BROOK

Brook was a Southerner, and the nicest man in Mine Hole. He was a respected, well-liked family man who worked like a dog to provide a decent home for his wife and five sons. He had little leisure time because he liked and needed money, and when he could, he'd put in long overtime hours — some 16-hour days.

"Times were tough down South," he told Cooke, the young boy hanging around the streets. "When my mother washed clothes, I had to haul buckets of water uphill a half a mile to the house. Man, it was really hard being a kid in those days. But I figured out how to carry five buckets of water at one time."

When Cooke doubted the story, Brook bragged, "I can carry five buckets at once and walk balancing myself on that railroad track right now. Believe me?"

Cooke said, "Don't believe it. Show me."

Brook suggested that they get five pails of water and meet at the railroad track. At the track, Brook grabbed one pail and balanced it on his head and carried two pails in each hand. He stepped up on the

Brook, a family man, was strong; he could lift one of these bales single handedly.

track, and, perfectly balancing himself, walked a good 100 feet before stepping off. Not a drop of water was spilled.

His body was like most men's bodies in Mine Hole. His 6-foot frame was covered with muscle. Because he was one of the toughest around he landed a coveted rare position in the paper mill — foreman in the stock house. The stock house was the section where the trains or trucks brought in the paper pulp and lime for making paper. The

45

pulp was in 1,500-pound bales and the lime in 200-pound bags. Brook was proud of his status — the first and the only colored on the foreman level. In fact, he was the highest-ranking colored person in either plant, and the plant had 1,200 folks around that time. Being a boss meant having power; and he liked to flex his muscles. It was also a way of getting those working under him to get moving and working harder. When the freight train pulled in, he'd be out there with his crew. He'd grab a 200-pound bag of lime under one arm and another 200-pound bag in the other arm and walk some 50 feet before putting them down inside the factory's storage area. He'd flip the 1,500-pound bales onto the hand trucks alone.

Brook had just put in a 16-hour day after a number of other 16-hour days. He stopped by Mrs. Town's for a drink before going home. On the way home, he fell asleep, drove right into the Sparkill Creek and drowned.

The shock of the sudden death of a fine, popular family man hit Mine Hole hard. The burial was in a quiet cemetery plot. In those days many burial plots met the guidelines of Jim Crow, coloreds in one section, whites in another.

GAMBLE

"Gamble, you're one no-good, cheatin' son of a bitch. I was watching you dealing the cards. Funny how you got four matching cards right off the top," said Dee-Troit.

Everyone knew he was telling the truth. They were being screwed in the game, one of many in Yummie's house. At that game were Gamble, Dee-Troit, Porkie Liver, Tiger Flowers, and an old man in his sixties named Will Turner. Will was not an everyday player, just a once-in-a-while player.

Will was a mild-mannered guy, medium build, still working in the mill. He rented a room on the first floor of the Pond Lily rooming house and was single but churchgoing. Luck was with him, and being that it was Saturday, he had a lot of time to play. While his luck was still with him, he thought he'd cut out of the game with $30, a lot of money. He didn't rush out the door, but hung around to eat Yummie's wife's cooking.

Night had fallen. Gamble had his eye on Will's money and he left the game, too. He figured no one would see him if he walked behind Pond Lily on the railroad tracks. Will's room was on the back and no one could see him enter. He went to the window of Will's room, tried it, and it wasn't locked. Pushing it open, he climbed in, closed it behind him, and crawled under the bed. Thirty dollars was $30 and Gamble could use the money. The rolls of dust under the bed didn't matter. He settled down quietly and waited.

Within the hour, Will came in thinking he'd get up for church the next day and share his winnings with God. Out from under the bed rolled Gamble. He jumped to his feet with an ice pick in hand and demanded the money. Will never let out a peep. Gamble went out the way he came in — $30 richer, no shame. Just a no-good mean nigger, thought Will. One of a few to break the Mine Hole rule: Don't go into a house to steal. A man's home is his castle.

Gamble carefully picked whom he was going to get tough with. He would not mess with super-tough Curlie, but a mild mannered guy like Foots would be bait for Gamble. Foots got this name because his feet were so bad he could hardly walk, but he could swim. Swimming was his thing, not fighting. Foots took a knife stabbing from Gamble and no one knew why. Gamble didn't need a reason — he was just damn mean.

Still, Gamble was a hard worker for the Lawsons. He was always on time. He first handled a team of horses and wagons hauling stone, lumber, sand, hay, corn, or whatever anyone needed. When the Lawsons switched from wagons to a truck, he was in seventh heaven. He chewed on a cigar, cap pulled down on his head, driving the truck with pride, feeling the power that a truck spelled out. He remained one of the Lawton's loyal workers for years.

The days of the horse and buggy were fading and automobiles were finding there way into Mine Hole. One of the first car owners was Tuttle, a really nice guy from the South. He worked hard and didn't hang out gambling, drinking, or fighting. He didn't waste money and therefore could afford a car. Owning a car meant you were really somebody of note, and Lil' Mabel had her eye on Tuttle.

Lil' Mabel was one of the prostitutes who lived in Mine Hole and was ready for service every day of the week. A small, brown-skinned woman, she was not bad-looking except she had the biggest butt in Mine Hole. It was wide, poked out and shook like a bowl of Jell-O when she walked down the street. That butt had a "come hither" look, and Lil' Mabel survived because it paid off, even during the Depression.

Lil' Mabel's ideas about colored women and sex were shaped down South. She had heard the stories of how women were raped on the slave ships and that the white plantation owners kept up the practice. Once in Mine Hole, working for white families, she kept her guard up, fearing the white man's advances. Lil' Mabel had a job working with an outstanding white family. One day while the wife was out shopping, the husband patted Lil' Mabel's big shaking butt, and that was the end of her doing domestic work. Turning a trick for money was better. She managed well.

Lil' Mabel was attracted to Tuttle for the car and money, but he didn't know Lil' Mabel was also seeing Gamble. Tuttle had gone hunting one day and was about to run out of gas, so he pulled up to the local gas station. He was short of cash. So he left his rifle with the gas station owner until he could get his money straight.

He drove down to Lil' Mabel's. The door was open, so he went in. Radio music was playing; the smell of "Midnight in Paris" perfume was strong. He had a feeling something was wrong. When he opened the bedroom door, there was Lil' Mabel and Gamble in bed. Gamble jumped up, grabbed his ice pick, and stabbed Tuttle several times. Tuttle staggered out of the house bleeding, climbed into his car, drove to the gas station, paid his debt, got his rifle, and got back into his car. He drove down to Lil' Mabel's, got out of the car, and blew the front door away. He shot out the windows but missed Gamble.

Getting weaker from losing blood, Tuttle drove himself to the hospital and survived, as usual. With all the shooting and cutting these tough guys went through, those bodies that had survived generation after generation of abuse didn't die.

Gamble didn't serve any prison time for the stabbing. Many coloreds felt the white policemen's attitude was, "Let 'em fight. Another nigger dead is another nigger I won't have to deal with."

HOWARD

It was late spring and the baseball season was just getting started when the usual gathering in J.B.'s barber shop was sounding off about whose team was the best. This discussion — mostly bragging — was heightened by the presence of three Jolly Nine baseball club members from Nanuet. The Jolly Nine was a colored club.

These Nanuet fellows were mainly members of well-established colored families in the county. They had 22 to 24 members from

The Mine Hole baseball team played near the mill. Howard, a top-flight center fielder, was a natural leader.

Spring Valley and Nanuet, a good place to practice, elected officers, beautiful white uniforms with black vertical stripes, and a great following. They had sponsors, including a legal redress lawyer from the NAACP. Their pitcher was outstanding and was paid for his service. Their games with other colored teams in Closter, Englewood and Haverstraw drew crowds.

Piermont's colored team was a mixed bag of migrants, old timers, and high schoolers. They had no regular, decent place to play or practice, used borrowed mismatched uniforms or bought them, had no officers and at best had only about 16 members.

Howard, a top-flight center fielder, was a natural leader and jealous of the Jolly Nine. In a braggadocious manner he said one day, "You know, Piermont can beat your asses any old time. How about Saturday afternoon? Winning team'll get $100." The game was on. Money in the game was a must. They'd make a wager and the losers would have to ante up the money.

In those days, the colored baseball leagues were just getting into full gear. There had been a few colored individuals going back to the 1850s on white teams, but they were passing for white or Indian or something. Over time and into the '20s and '30s, the coloreds got into a big business operation in their own leagues. Two or three of these league teams would come to Nyack to play at night under the lights and, boy, what a crowd would turn out. Real excitement from teams like the Brooklyn Giants, the Cuban All Stars and the Homestead Grays. Folks came from everywhere. Seeing players like these made others want to get in the act — be important, make money, better than construction or working in the mill. These players were role models to use a 20th century term. Role models for the Jolly Nine and Piermont teams.

Howard was at every game. He loved baseball — could catch and throw with the best. He was an athletic type, not muscle-bound, but quick and smart. He knew the game inside and out.

Leaving the barber shop, out in the road Howard began recruiting his ragtag team for the big event. They had not played the local white team yet — an annual event on the white team's very nice field. They'd get in a couple of practices in the school yard and planned to meet Saturday at noon for the trip to Nanuet.

Everyone was on time, climbed into cars, and when they got to Nanuet, had a little warm-up time. What a nice field it was — the grass was cut, the markers and bases were shining bright, and a grandstand for the loyal followers was filled to overflowing. It was a beautiful day and the spirit was heightened by the possibility of winning and getting some money.

The Jolly Nine team looked good, confident. Their playing mirrored the great investment of practice time, talent and commitment. Piermont, though ragged, was equally committed, talented and hungry for a win. Cooke, a high school pitcher, was in rare form. He fanned 19 of the Jolly Niners. Howard, Cooke, and others got some runs and beat the Jolly Niners with a score of 6-1. An unforgettable event..

Howard was a go-getter on all levels. A skilled craftsman, he could do a little carpentry, paint, and fix anything around a house. He developed his own business and hired a few guys who worked with him on a regular basis. They even traveled down to Jersey to work. It followed a pattern reaching back into slavery days. Enslaved craftsmen were often able to buy their freedom and travel everywhere. Craftsmen in slavery were hired out by the master and had a higher status than the plantation-bound slave. They worked around the house rather than the field and there developed two groups of coloreds — "house niggers" and "field niggers." Those in the house thought themselves better than those in the fields.

Howard was more of the "house nigger" type, and his family was his pride. A good provider, he really liked being in charge in his household of six children. They had plenty of good food and were nicely dressed, and he cared about their getting along and getting ahead in life. His wife, a southerner as well, was a good homemaker, mother, and wife.

But there was something else about Howard — one woman was not enough for this man. Mine Hole had a mixture of whites and colored living side by side. There were good friends living side by side as well. Whites didn't play skin, but they'd play craps — outdoors. They didn't come indoors into the regular gathering places like church, Mrs. Town's, Yummie's, the barber shop or the pool hall. They came indoors into private homes, sharing baby sitting and concern when there was trouble. There were solid white and colored friendships in Mine Hole.

Howard and Mike, who was white, were really good friends. They were in and out of each other's homes often, but Mike was a workaholic and put in double shifts in the mill because he loved money.

Howard was like a member of the family and came into Mike's house and enjoyed the good cooking of Mike's wife, Vickie, especially her baking. Her bread pudding was outstanding, with custard on the bottom and the bread on the top. It wasn't like the colored bread pudding, which was heavy like a cornbread — a wet solid mass of custard, bread and raisins. Vickie's was the best.

Vickie had a beautiful face and long, flowing chestnut-colored hair which she let loose when not cooking or cleaning. Her body was not soft and flabby, but full and ready. Old Mike was for action, but with all that hard work in the mill and putting in double shifts, everyone knew he could not keep Vickie happy.

Howard was in and out of that house all of the time. Being an athletic type and only working a normal day meant he had the energy to run after and satisfy women. Some even said Mike probably liked the fact that Howard would do what Mike couldn't do.

Race mixing went on all the time in Mine Hole. The Howard-Vickie affair was the best known and seemed like a daily thing. Others had other plans. A colored person and a white person would get on the bus at different stops and remain separated. The bus would travel down the Jersey side, drive onto the ferry at Fort Lee and across 125th Street, stopping at the Hotel Theresa at Seventh Avenue.

That was a really well run, large, attractive hotel. Many colored celebrities came in and out of the place. It was a kind of mecca of colored upper-class tourists.

The union between Mine Hole coloreds and whites within the walls of the Hotel Theresa were filled with fun and passion. They didn't include arguments, fighting, and cutting. They didn't include marriage, either.

HARRY PALMER

Ever hear the one about the fellow and girl who had their wedding date set? The girl, feeling a little frisky, snuggled up to the guy and suggested she didn't want to wait until the wedding to make love. He said, "It won't be long until July, why can't we wait?' She asked, 'How long will it be by July?'"

That's him, Harry Palmer, telling his jokes again. He was always telling jokes, and somehow you'd just smile when you saw him. You'd remember some joke he told you the last time you saw him, or you figured he was going to tell you another good one in a few minutes.

Harry was slim, about 5 feet 6 inches, light-skinned, with good hair, and worked in construction. Not a recent immigrant, his family lived in the county.

Harry lived in Mine Hole with his wife from Hillburn and a couple of children. One of them became a teacher of horseback riding. Colored folks didn't take lessons on how to ride a horse, so this son moved into white, moneyed circles where he earned a damn good living. He eventually taught a white woman so well her husband left and Harry's son moved in and lived with her happily ever after.

It was the drinking and gambling that put Harry right in the middle of the action in Mine Hole. He could drink, but handled everything with a few jokes. No need to fight — tell a joke, and for him it worked. Didn't have all of the muscle of the guys from the South, so he avoided fights. Smart.

Back in those days, walking was the way to get from one place to another. So a three- to five-mile walk after work wasn't unusual. Harry and friends were walking home from a construction job in Closter and he was as loud as usual. All of a sudden a pain hit him in the gut and he had to "go."

"Go on — I'll catch up" he said. Luck was with him, he thought. There's an empty house with an outhouse. That one didn't empty into the creek, but hung over a deep, deep hole. His friends went on and Harry slipped inside the outhouse. Looked like it hadn't been used for a bit. Cobwebs everywhere. The pages of a Sears Roebuck catalogue in it were yellow with age. There was a seat over a deep hole, but it too was cobwebbed and dusty. No time to clean it up. He had to go. So he stepped up on the side of the board that held the seat, figuring on squatting rather than sitting. This is a case where being too clean didn't pay off. The board was rotten. It broke. Harry fell in.

Don't know the details of how he got out, but he was loaded, covered up to his chest, stinking but surviving. No place to really clean up, so he walked into Mine Hole. Embarrassed and angry, he got to Mrs. Town's

where he knew his friends were drinking and gambling. There he was, the walking jokester, full of shit as usual. They hosed him down. His friends came out, and Harry was the biggest laugh of a lifetime.

The next afternoon was a hot Saturday and down the pier a group

Harry Palmer fell into an outhouse like this.

Courtesy Al Durtschi, E-Mail: mark@waltonfeed.com

of guys went for a swim. There was Greasy, Dee-Troit, Gamble and Harry. They stripped off all their clothes and were enjoying the cool, clean, Hudson River water. They dove in, swimming around a bit, horsing around a bit. Along came three white women, wanting to cool off, too. They kept a distance and kept fully clothed, but their bathing suits were wet, clinging and revealing. There was no talking between the groups. Each kept its distance, but action speaks louder than words. Slowly, quietly Harry's body was like a thermometer — the heat of excitement caused it to rise. All the guys saw it. The "thang" kept getting longer, longer and longer. The biggest in all of Mine Hole.

The two things Harry was remembered for were his humor and his physical endowment. The second put him into a very privileged class. Among all the men he held the undisputed championship.

CARRI

"**N**ew York, that's for me," Carri told her sister, Mattie. "You know, you've heard they's plenty of jobs, high livin' and I can meet me a man who's making money, too."

Mattie added, "But we live pretty good. Lucky for us that old white man Tucker really loved Grandma and left her 500 acres and a house"

Carri interrupted to say, "But life on a farm ain't life up North. Cousin Bill in Piermont says he can get me plenty a work with white folks. Wages are better. I'm 20 now and I'm leavin'."

Those were the thoughts running around Carri's head, so she got her few things together. She put a rabbit's foot in her pocketbook for good luck. Her momma made her a lunch of fried chicken, cornbread, and a couple of apples, and she rode away on the train.

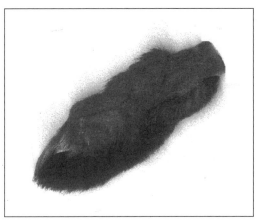

A rabbit's foot for good luck was Carri's charm. They were good then and the luck of the rabbit's foot continues today.

Once in Piermont, she only spent two days in a room Bill got for her, because she got a good job with a wealthy Piermont white family — the Van Nyeses. Carri thought about the fact the husband in the family might want to get fresh, but decided she'd take a chance, because that didn't happen in every family. Maybe luck would be with her. She'd pray on it. God answers prayers and she had her rabbit's foot.

It was easy for Carri to get a job. She was a fairly attractive, light-brown-skinned woman, with nice hair, about 5 foot 6 inches tall, well built with a smiling, open face. She was young and could put in a good day's work.

Carri did a good job of washing, ironing, cooking, cleaning, taking care of two children, and nursing anyone in the family when they got sick. Not lazy a bit, she got to be a fond, trusted family friend. She worried when Mr. Van Nyes began coming home too late for dinner, and when he was missing a night ever so often. Carri also worried when Junior was not getting his numbers. In her couple of years with the Van Nyeses, Carri could and did offer advice, just like a family member.

There was time off, every Thursday and every other Sunday. Sunday off was after breakfast and in time for church. Carri loved the services at St. Charles, meeting the people. On Thursdays after breakfast, she'd go up to Nyack and shop. She'd send money home, take in a movie, grab a snack or two at Woolworth's. But when the sun began to go down, she'd head on back to Piermont and to Mrs. Town's. She got stuck on meeting Charlie Avery there. Charlie hadn't been there long. He was a cousin to Dee-Troit and worked at the mill. He was kind of quiet, a good looking big, muscle-bound guy like the others from the South. He and Carri got something going between them, and he didn't talk marrying because he had a legal wife down South.

"You've done spent enough time waitin' on dem white folks," he said. "Quit. Come live wif me and you won't have to kiss they ass anymore. We can get us an apartment here in Mine Hole and you won't have to work any more."

Carri couldn't believe her ears. "Not work any more." Well, she'd be willing to take in laundry or do some day's work. She'd be home to fix dinner, keep house, have children, and keep him cozy and warm every night in bed.

Tearfully, she left the family and took up living with Charles. They had an apartment on the second floor and were doing fine for a year or so. Then Charles' drinking got out of hand.

Drunk as a coot, one morning after an all-night drinking and gambling session, Charlie staggered in and woke Carri up looking for a fight. He was tough enough to beat up many a guy in Mine Hole and Carri was no match for him. She saw the writing on the wall, jumped out of the bed screaming, and was about to run out of the house when he hit her and she fell down the outside concrete stairs. Screaming in Mine Hole was common, but it was usually part of the Saturday night music. These morning screams were less common and folks took notice and some came out to see. Charlie grabbed her hair and pulled her back up those concrete stairs by her hair first and by her head. One awful sight. In a couple of days, he'd quit Carri and Mine Hole, never to be seen again.

She'd made up her mind she wouldn't go back to domestic work. It was too much fun being with colored people full time. She could make it on her own. She could keep on laundering, doing day work and a little light bed action for money. One month, she was short of cash and thought a house rent party was the best answer. It was one of the best money making ideas around for paying rent.

It was her first party. She passed the word that the party would be Saturday night and the food would be good — fried chicken, collards, cornbread, sweet potato pie, bread pudding, and chitterlings.

Carri's place was always clean so she only had to cook the food, get the corn liquor from Sam Boston, and borrow a few chairs. Her Victrola worked well and she had some good records, including Bessie Smith, Fletcher Henderson and Louis Armstrong. If everyone had enough to drink and eat and the joint would be jumping The more you drank, the more you'd dance; cutting the fool was the idea. Having a ball. Put in a small fight or two — here and there. Collect the money and the rent would be paid until the next month.

Carri couldn't make enough on house rent parties, day work, and laundering. She got hooked up with one guy after another, nothing steady. They all beat her up and she kept coming back for more. In a short while, she became another "prostitute in residence" and her customers were colored and white.

One colored guy looking for sport arranged a paid-for-view peep session for those wanting to see Carri hooked up with a lesbian for hire. Mine Hole had a new piece of fat to chew on — the Carri-lesbian affair. An event not to be forgotten.

This didn't prove to be Carri's choice because she really continued to spend most of her time with men. Prostitution, day work, ironing, and house rent parties sustained her. She managed well enough not to return to the seeming security of the family home down South.

J.B.

Not every migrant from the South who landed in Mine Hole was big, muscular, loud, and wrong like Dee-Troit and Gamble. The people of Mine Hole were a varied group and many were from around Roxbury and Oxford, North Carolina, with names like Brown, Cunningham, Tuck, Greene, and Bullock. Migrants of any color followed family and friends who got to the Promised Land first. That's why there were so many Swedes in Minnesota, Jamaicans in Brooklyn, Dutch in New York, and Irish in Manhattan. Someone paved the way for others to come later. J.B., who followed the crowd from North Carolina, wasn't the rowdy type and brought skills and a business sense with him. He could have gotten that from his forefathers, since there was a large

A gathering place for cutting hair; all types of conversation; agreements and disagreements. J.B.'s barber shop was Mine Hole's listening post and debate forum.

number of free coloreds who were in the trades and in business for themselves. Some slaves knew trades like carpentry, iron work, and masonry.

Whatever J.B.'s background, he was a man who showed intelligence, dignity, poise, and confidence. He was about 6 feet 2 inches, straight as an arrow, rich brown skin, sharp features, and a lovely grade of hair. J.B. had a barber shop in Mine Hole for a number of years. He owned the business as well as his home and provided well for his family. Not one to gamble or take too many nips of corn liquor or run after women, he was really a respected man.

A straight razor is a dangerous looking thing. This bare piece of steel was almost 6 inches long and an inch wide and attached at one end was a tight fitting cover of leather. In those days, every barber's chair had attached a broad leather strop, about 4 inches wide and about 2 feet long. It was used for sharpening the razor. The barber would hold the end of the strop out and slap the opened razor against the leather strop several times to sharpen it. Of course, those who shaved themselves at home had the same thing. The razor was also a deadly weapon too often used in a fight. No one was going to trust their face and neck to a drunken, crazy man with a blade like that. That's one reason J.B. was a successful barber. Men really put their lives in his hands when they sat in his chair. They felt safe.

The barber shop was a place to talk about the numbers, women, fighting, hunting, who's running with whom, the colored baseball leagues, and Joe Louis. You could find out anything about a town from keeping your ears open in the barber shop. Sometimes a shop would have a back room for gambling; up front there might be a couple of guys playing checkers.

Some barber shops had a bootblack stand. It was a place where the bootblacks would bring the rustiest of shoes to a high polish using the best of polish, dressing, and a little spit. The customer would climb up on a platform that held a comfortable armchair and put his feet on the elevated foot supports. The bootblack would slap the soft polishing cloth so quickly it sometimes seemed to make music. The sporting types like Yummie or Pop Smith would get a professional shoe shine anytime. Others came mainly on the weekend.

The barber shop really took up a lot of J.B.'s time, but he loved to hunt and to practice his skill as a sharpshooter. He was the best in Mine Hole, and maybe the best in the county, the state, and beyond. He loved showing off to the kids hanging around the street. Everyone knew not to mess with J.B., because if he aimed his shotgun in your direction, you were a dead duck.

One of his favorite ways to practice was to put a small bottle cap on the railroad track, walk across the

AP/ Wide World

Joe Louis, the great heavyweight boxing champion, in the 1930s. Mine Holers admired him as a colored millionaire who made it out of poverty and to the top.

street to his yard about 50 feet away, and turn his back to the tracks. Then he'd rest a rifle barrel on his shoulder facing the bottle cap and, with a mirror on the butt he'd take aim and pull the trigger and knock the cap off every time.

But J.B. wasn't about to resort to gunfire when a loud drunk came by his house raising hell, being a general nuisance. J.B. neither used a deadly razor nor his gun. He quietly made a fist, hit the guy like a professional prizefighter, and knocked him the hell out. Quietly, deadly, he dusted off his hands and closed the door after him when he went inside.

ROCK

"**I**f you're white, you're right. If you're brown, get down. If you're black, get back." That was a common colored saying in those days. And that's the way many coloreds felt about themselves. They felt they'd be better off if they were white, and they'd do anything to look the part. Having a conchaleen was one step in that direction, because a conchaleen was a way to have straight hair. The conchaleen king in Mine Hole was Rock, a barber in J.B.'s shop. Man, he could do a mean conchaleen, and was the best in Mine Hole.

Rock was the second barber in the J.B.'s shop. He had a steady stream of customers and did the conchaleen for those with real money. The conchaleen made the woolly hair straight by mixing lye and grease on the hair, washing it out and repeating the process. Lye was used as a cleaning product because it ate away dirt. It could be powerful and dangerous. Lye was used in fights. Once the hair was straightened, Rock worked on waving and curling it since having it dead straight was not stylish. He might use a hot curling iron for the curls. He might use a cold thick wave set popular with white hair dressers. Flat waves were the style and a stocking cap did a good job of holding the flat waves in place. A second system was the "doo-rag," a cap with a string through it. Pull on the string for a tight fit.

Rock had gained a lot of respect in the area over time. He came from the western part of the county. A short stocky, dark-skinned guy, generally he was a bit sullen with little to say. He was finishing up a conchaleen job when a Hillburn guy, drunk as a coot, staggered into the shop. Hillburn was about 17 miles west of Mine Hole and known for its beautiful, exotic women. They were from a mixture of the Ramapo Indians, Hessian soldiers and the Dutch. Added to that mixture were the coloreds who got into the act somewhere along the way. Some say light-skinned Hillburn folks thought they were better than dark-skinned folks.

When the Hillburn guy staggered in, he was rocking and rolling and shadow boxing. It was a busy time of the day, the place was crowded, and Rock was finishing up a conchaleen and had no time for that kind of nonsense.

"Man - why don't you move on down the street?" Rock said, to which the drunk replied, "Don't tell me what to do, nigger. Step outside."

Rock did just that and in a second a crowd gathered. The drunk took one swing at Rock. Rock didn't bother to use the lye on the shelf or a steel razor. His closest companion was his switchblade knife, strapped to his leg in a leather case under his pants. He quickly took it out, held it high in the air, and brought it down on the man's shoulder with such force it almost cut the arm off. The blood was everywhere. The ambulance came and took the guy to the hospital and he recovered. Rock ran down the street and hid. When he was caught and tried, he spent six months in jail.

While investigating the case, three white policemen came to Cooke's house and tried to bully their way inside. He was only 14 years old at the time, but he was smart and asked for a warrant. They didn't have one of course — just thought being white was enough. They turned around and left.

Some folks wondered Rock didn't use the lye or the razor in the attack. Most figured he didn't want to hurt business.

CORNBREAD AND GREASY

Fighting in Mine Hole was a way of life. Everyone knew how to make a point — just roll up your fist and hit whoever was bothering you. Talk was cheap. It took up too much time. And some folks just got a thrill out of fighting. For instance, a group of hefty colored guys would go to a local Irish bar just to pick a fight. They'd go in and get served easily because Piermont didn't practice Jim Crow in public places, not like Nyack. Those guys would get a couple of "cluckers" (any strong alcoholic drink) under their belt. They'd listen to the juke box a bit and then they'd pass some remarks about the "Shanty Irish." That was it. Another bloody fist fight was on — no weapons, just fists between men in a man's world.

It was one thing to fight at a bar, but inside or outside Mine Hole, alcohol was fuel for fighting. It helped the guys lose all the wariness of being away from home and their family 'way down South. Living in a room wasn't easy. Being colored wasn't easy, either. And drinking was the social thing to do. It was important to see who could drink the most. What brand of liquor you drank could tell a story about you. Some could afford liquor, some wine, and some home brew beer. No one would stop drinking. It felt too good.

Fighting was so popular that it was only natural that some of the best fighters would end up in the semipro ring. The best ring was down in Jersey. Among those going to Jersey were Soldier Boy, J.B., Dee-Troit, Cornbread, and Greasy. The guys standing up in the ring the longest would get the most pay.

Cornbread and Greasy were in that class. They'd still be standing even though their eyes were bloody and sometimes shut, and they had cuts over their eyebrows. They'd have wobbly knees and would be rocking and rolling, but they knew not to let their butt hit the canvas, because when it did it was like hitting a time clock. The pay was over.

Both guys were heavyweights. Cornbread weighed about 220

pounds, and stood 6 feet 2 inches. Greasy was the same height, very dark skinned, and weighed about 250 pounds. One time they were gambling at a pick-up game. They had been drinking and Cornbread was looking for a fight.

"Greasy, your momma's got dirty drawers," he said.

Talk about anyone's momma was called playing the "dirty dozens," and was the lowest of low insults. That fight began right at the gambling table, continued onto the porch, and finally into the street. A crowd gathered quickly. The fists were flying, blood flowing, and they were about even by professional ring standards. Sometimes Greasy was on the bottom, and they'd change positions. Sometimes Cornbread on the bottom. At one point when Cornbread was on the bottom and Greasy was pounding his head on the cement sidewalk, through his bloody eyes, Cornbread saw an ax leaning against the steps. He quickly changed his tune began to cry crocodile tears.

"Greasy — you're the greatest, I'm sorry I lied about your momma. Man I've had enough. I give up. You've won." Greasy was sucked in. He got up, the proud winner, and was about to strut for the crowd when Cornbread grabbed the ax and started chasing him. Up the mountain, onto 9W, and lucky for Greasy, a New York City bus was standing there and the door was open for a passenger. He jumped on, the door closed. He never came back to Mine Hole.

It was 30 years later when Cooke was in Harlem at Club Baron socializing.

He heard a familiar voice call out questioningly "Cooke?" It was Greasy, looking handsome and well put together. He had a manager-bouncer job there. Guess you'd say he won out after all.

DEAFEY

Deafey's steady girlfriend was the wife of a man who was a big shot at St. Charles and who worked at the mill at night. It was very convenient for Deafey to sneak in and get a little bit, sneak out and go

Deafey was a handsome outdoorsman who knew intimately the terrain for 10 miles around, and every stripe, every feather.

to sleep in his little shack at the Grays' homestead. He lived there in a cabin all year round for many years. He was the gardener, tended the chickens, did repairs, and cleaned up, but one of his biggest jobs was cutting down the trees on the property for firewood. They had a huge house, and keeping it warm meant a lot of work.

Deafey was up to the task. A big tough guy, about 200 pounds, 5 feet 11 inches, he had plenty of muscle and walked with a limp. He was totally deaf, but he was a master at reading lips. He really was a marvel at cutting down trees alone. He used a rip saw, an ax, iron wedges, and sledge hammer. He'd fell the trees, trim them, cut the pieces up into fireplace size, and neatly pile them into four-foot high stacks up near the house. While one stack of wood would get smaller, another two or three would be waiting and ready. Might seem like a simple thing, but it kept Deafey hopping. The joy for him was that he didn't have to work inside a mill. He could do this job and it was all outdoors, all year long.

His real love was hunting. Deer, rabbit, raccoon, and possum were hunted and muskrats were trapped. The fur brought nice money and the eating was choice. During the Depression, Deafey kept many a family from starving with his prizes from hunting.

Deafey had a 10-gauge shotgun with 32-inch double barrels. He'd choose the size of the shot according to the size of animal he was going for. He'd also have to think about how far away the animal might be. The lead shot would scatter inside the animal. The person cooking it had to pick it out first.

As a hunter, Deafey knew much about nature and warmly shared it with Cooke. He knew the different plants and bushes, how to use them for medicine if you got sick. He knew the habits of animals, which ones washed their foods before eating them, which animals slept during the day. Having walked all over while hunting, he knew where the foundations of many old buildings were. In Skunk Hollow, a section where free colored once lived, he could point out the foundations of houses, the wells, and where the gardens had been. The man had so much knowledge.

Deafey had schooled Cooke well in the art of hunting and said he knew the path of the biggest deer around. They would shoot it. They cleaned and oiled their guns the night before and early the next morning they set out for the area near Route 303. They had it all worked out. Cooke would be down in the swamp and Deafey, who had read the pathway right from the deer tracks, would be up on the hill. The two hunters were about 200 feet apart. Cooke flushed out the big, prize-sized deer from the woods and screamed and yelled at Deafey, pointing to the deer. To no avail. Deafey, stone deaf, heard nothing. He was looking in another direction and the deer passed him up the hill within 50 feet. He never saw him.

SOLDIER BOY

The buzzards' roost was the public place where coloreds had to sit apart from white people. It was a segregated public area. It was an area that Jim Crow had set aside, saying no whites could use — just those who were black, less than human — like buzzards. Buzzards' roosts were usually elevated. In the 1930s, in the U.S.A., the movies of Birmingham, Atlanta, and Nyack had buzzards' roosts, elevated balconies just for coloreds.

Cooke, Soldier Boy, and Dodie wanted to see Tom Mix at the Nyack movie. The fact that they'd have to use the buzzards' roost

The ukulele was as popular years ago as the guitar is today, and the price was right when funds were short in Mine Hole.

probably never crossed their minds. Coloreds learned to live in two worlds — colored and white. "Man just go along with the go-along," they'd say. Only a few would never go along with Jim Crow.

Nyack was a half step ahead of the South. Down South you paid your money and entered the movie by an alley way, beside or behind the theater. In Nyack, you paid your money to the white cashier in the front and then walked in the front to the inside stairs to the buzzards' roost.

The bus ran through Piermont, but Grand View, a half mile away, was in another fare zone, and from that point the fare to Nyack was only a nickel. So these colored fellows usually walked through Piermont into Grand View, one wealthy, lily-white town. Cooke, 15 years old, was carrying his ukulele and it hit a bush and out onto the street fell a gold chain. They all stopped and saw two other pieces of jewelry hanging on the bushes and they called up to a white woman on the porch, "Is this your stuff?" The woman didn't answer. She said nothing, went inside, and called the police. They later learned that a few minutes before they appeared she had walked into her house when a robbery was in progress. The burglar dropped some of the jewelry as he ran away.

Quick as a flash, the lone policemen arrived from Grand View and the fellows gave up the jewelry. Soldier Boy kept one piece. On to the theater the fellows went.

Around nine o'clock, when the show was over, Cooke had a curfew and had to get home. He left the others to catch the bus. His bus met a roadblock of Piermont and Grand View police. The police removed Cooke from the bus and took him to the Grand View police station. The police tried to pressure Cooke to say his friend was the burglar. They failed. The others had been picked up at the park and taken to the police station, where the police added another colored guy named John for good measure.

In the police station, Soldier Boy was singled out. The police put a big coat on him, turned up the collar, and put a hat on him which they pulled down on one side. They obviously wanted to obscure who he was. Then they called in the woman.

"The robber was taller," she said. "This isn't the guy."

Those four weren't even the big brute types we've written about before. They weren't a threat to the policemen. Soldier Boy, always in army surplus clothes, was a dark-skinned fellow of about 150 pounds, 5 feet 7 inches. His pockmarked face, probably from smallpox, made him unattractive. He worked hard, was a boxer, and walked like Charlie Chaplin. His buddy John was only 5 feet 3 inches, dark-skinned, bowlegged and stocky. The other two, Buddy and Cooke, were school-age.

In the police station, the cops really gave them a work over — blows with fists, blows from rubber hoses, slamming them against the floor and/or the walls. It was horrible, but somehow Cooke was spared, possibly because his aunt babysat in one of the policemen's families. At midnight when he was not home, his family came to check it out. He was unharmed.

The others were battered, bruised, silenced, humiliated, and intimidated. They were released. Soldier Boy spent six months in jail awaiting trial. He was released when the white woman, again, said the burglar was taller than Soldier Boy. He lost six months of his life, his salary, and his dignity.

EPILOGUE

A majority of the Mine Holers of the 1920s and 1930s that we have written about are dead and gone. Most died right here in Mine Hole. They were among the many who helped build America. They worked hard in the mill and in construction. They provided the muscle for the highways, bridges, and many of the buildings which stand today. They were the strong who survived.

They created a raucous climate, but they were very respectful of the neighborhood children and churchgoing adults, never cursing in front of them. When report cards came out, some would ask to see children's grades and drop them a few coins of encouragement along with their kind words. "Make something out of yourself."

Those moving up, who had Mine Hole roots, included school teachers, a public school principal, a college professor, a commissioner of Human Rights, social workers, and policemen. One was nominated for a Pulitzer Prize in music. Leonard Cooke, our griot, has many citations, including an honorary doctorate from a local college.

Many are gone, gone but not forgotten. There is an old expression, "Laughing to keep from crying." Hearing the stories repeated is part of how the black man has survived the pain over the years. The recall of events and the laughter are tension-releasing mechanisms. It made it possible to survive then and the retelling gives relief today. We have made some progress, but we have not yet arrived. The pain is still here and we still have a way to go as a race of people. The process of laughing and feeling relief has fueled our personal need to share this piece of history with others.

But, lest we forget, someone said, "The survival of the human spirit is faith-filled."

THE MINE HOLE

A creek runs east from the Sparkill dam
with a rushing flow to the river.
A high hill on the north and one on the south
make the valley as pretty as ever.

Do you know what they called that pretty place,
ever since I was a child?
Sure we knew it was a ghetto, you lived a fast pace
. . . . and wild.

The newspaper named us the "Mine Hole" —
from Boss's butcher shop to Comfort Coal,
But we had an integrated neighborhood
without planning to make that our goal.

71

We had Irish, Italian, Polish, German,
Indian and Spanish, too.
It was far safer than today's living
because of what the people would do.

We never had to lock our doors.
We all were poor together.
Some would steal coal from Comfort Coal
and help others keep warm in cold weather.

They had great respect for old folks here,
and respect for the children, too.
If you cursed when Mom was coming from church,
they would beat you black and blue.

Everyone seemed to have a nickname;
some were funny as could be.
They were easy to remember,
but their real names you'd never see.

There was "Tiger Flowers" (about six foot four)
with a nasty stab wound on his face.
There was "Pop Smith" (six feet by six feet wide)
with feet too big to give chase.

There was Bob Powell (about three hundred pounds),
who considered himself a smooth talker.
There was "Soldier Boy" (about five feet eight)
but we knew his last name was Walker.

There were "Little Red," "Big Red," and "Little Pop," too.
These names we all remember.
For they were a part of our neighborhood
for January through each December.

They gambled almost any time
especially Friday, Saturday, and Sunday.
The house parties started on Thursday night
and lasted through to Monday.
Fried chicken, potato salad, and greens
was the menu many nights,
But if you didn't have pigs' feet
that party wouldn't be right.

I could go right on forever,
for the "Mine Hole" will always be
Imbedded deep within
my fondest memory.

By Leonard C. Cooke

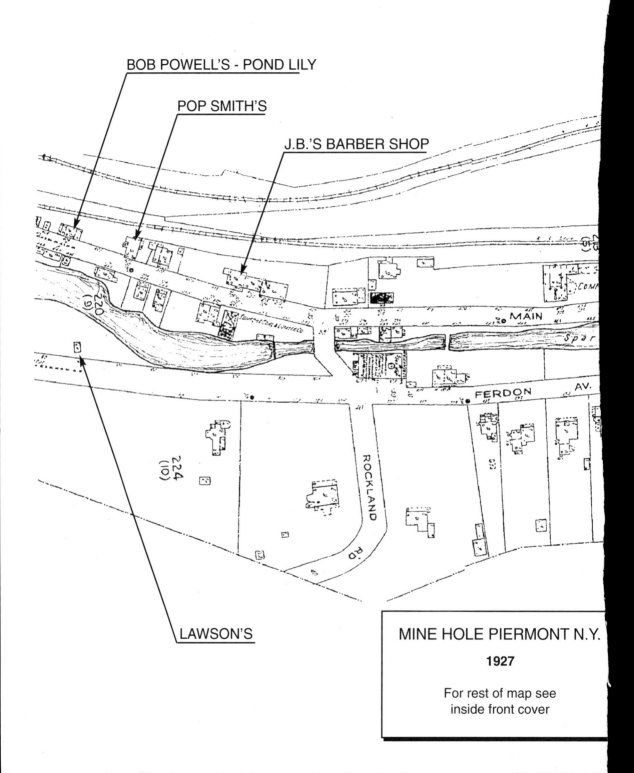

BOB POWELL'S - POND LILY

POP SMITH'S

J.B.'S BARBER SHOP

220
(9)

224
(10)

MAIN

Spar

FERDON AV.

ROCKLAND RD.

LAWSON'S

MINE HOLE PIERMONT N.Y.

1927

For rest of map see
inside front cover

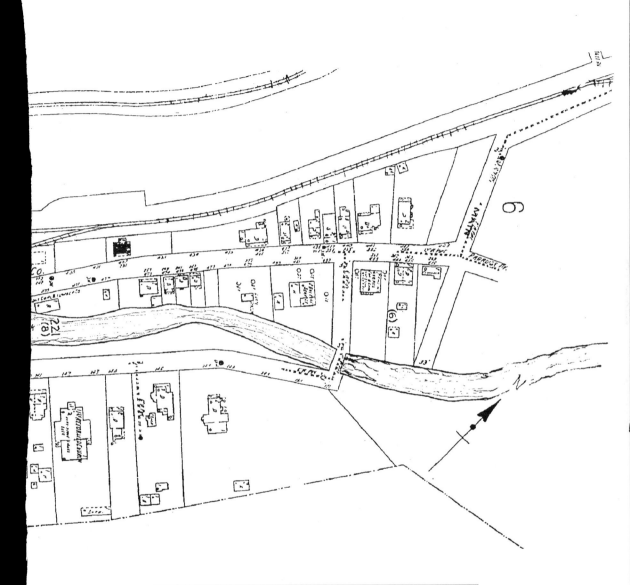

The section of the Sparkill Creek that runs through the Village of Piermont was once known as the "slote." This map shows the Mine Hole area located on the northeast bank of the slote — west of the center of the village.